MAGICAL CLASSROOM

MAGICAL CLASSROOM

CREATING EFFECTIVE, BRAIN-FRIENDLY ENVIRONMENTS FOR LEARNING

F. NOAH GORDON

Zephyr
Press

REACHING THEIR HIGHEST POTENTIAL

Tucson, Arizona

Zephyr Press
Tucson, Arizona

Magical Classroom
Creating Effective, Brain-Friendly Environments for Learning

All ages

© 1995 by Zephyr Press
Printed in the United States of America

ISBN 1-56976-020-9

Editors: Stacey Lynn and Stacey Shropshire
Design and production: Daniel Miedaner

Zephyr Press
P.O. Box 66006
Tucson, Arizona 85728-6006

Library of Congress Cataloging-in-Publication Data

Printed on recycled paper

DEDICATION

MAY THEIR TEACHINGS
BE OUR TEACHINGS

This book is dedicated to indigenous peoples, especially to friends and teachers among Native Americans, New Zealand Maoris, and Australian Aboriginal peoples. These people's gifts to us are carried within their oral traditions, which offer philosophy, cosmology, and approaches to the important questions that European-derived cultures continue to ask. The native peoples understand that all is one consciousness, expressed in infinite ways and forms. They grasp the principle that the physical universe seemingly outside of us is intimately connected with us through our actions, thoughts, and feelings. Their cosmology teaches reverence for all life forms. Their educative models are designed to help the learner know her or his relationship with self, family, and tribe, and to see relationships beyond and with animal and plant kingdoms. As with many Eastern cultures, they teach us to find that center within, from which all knowing comes, and to know that it is who we are at that center that carries its influence beyond our bodies.

Fred Noah Gordon
Minneapolis, Minnesota

CONTENTS

INTRODUCTION

This book is about a way of learning and a way of teaching that is based primarily on brain research as well as on principles of physics, medicine, sports training, and other disciplines concerned with how the brain learns and creates behavior. The message coming to us from this research is that we are far more creative, intelligent, and capable of expanded learning and performance than most of us ever dreamed possible. Further, this capacity for expanded living constitutes our *natural state,* our *natural neurologic heritage.* Operating from this expanded state, we can solve problems readily and efficiently, access lateral thinking processes, bring meaning to our personal lives, attune to artistic inspiration, improve our physical health, discover that we have a wonderful memory, and improve athletic and other body performance.

This is the good news. The bad news is that few of us ever realize the great gifts of this heritage. Why should this be so? Might schools become places where people can learn to access and benefit from our apparently vast and perhaps unlimited capacities?

This research sets the stage for showing how classroom learning environments *can* help students effectively tap their fuller brain faculties in order to take charge of managing their personal lives and to feel happy and fulfilled in the process.

The classroom approaches advocated here will be new to some readers, familiar to many, and usable by all. The concepts from which these approaches have emerged have been expressed in modern times by educators such as John Dewey, Jean Piaget, Maria Montessori, Rudolph Steiner, Reuven Feuerstein, Moshe Feldenkrais, Georgi Lozanov, Fritjof Capra, Gregory Bateson, Kenneth and Rita Dunn, Renatta and Geoffrey Caine, D. T. Suzuki, and Abraham Maslow. Educators have applied the concepts successfully, with demonstrated and often dramatic results (Caine and Caine 1991; Gardner 1983; Lozanov 1978; Marzano 1988; Schuster and Gritton 1986).

THE PURPOSE OF EDUCATION

Research shows that memorizing the names of state capitals, studying the structure of a cell, and even learning to read and work simple math problems are of limited value to learners and are accomplished with low efficiency unless viewed by the learners to be *useful* and *applicable* to their *current* life *interests* and *needs.* This book offers the view that the task of schooling is to address students' motivation to successfully manage their daily life adventures, challenges, interests, and needs. You are invited to consider how curriculum designed to serve these tasks can best emerge from a focus on real-life problem-solving strategies and processes. Curriculum *content* can then offer tools that are timely and relevant to students and that students can take immediately into their daily world.

1

MODEL, MODEL, WHO MADE THE MODEL?

ASSUMPTIONS OF TRADITIONAL LEARNING

What goes on every day in tens of thousands of classroom settings has its foundations in long-held assumptions about learning. What are some of these assumptions? From what larger cultural context did they emerge? What is now changing in that larger context that is generating *new* assumptions about what constitutes brain-friendly environments?

Further, what school-based learning methods are emerging from this change and which ones are proving successful? And finally, how can you, as an educator, become an even more effective facilitator of learning by helping to create environments that are increasingly supportive of your students' natural and preferred learning processes?

To begin, let's look at three examples from which our current assumptions and models have developed. We start in the mid-1800s, move to the time of the "Scientific Revolution," and end with a model that emerged on the scene about fifty years ago and now operates powerfully in our daily lives.

ASSUMPTION MAKER 1: THE FACTORY MODEL

We might cringe if people suggest that schools are in any way like factories, yet our present educational model is closely related to the factory system of the early and mid 1800s. The challenge of that time was to design learning settings to facilitate integration and job preparation for hundreds of thousands of immigrants from diverse cultural backgrounds. The assumptions behind this system were clear, and their expression can still be found in many contemporary classrooms, especially at the secondary and postsecondary levels worldwide:

1. We can identify the skill base that will be required of our students upon graduation and into a projected future.
2. To best accomplish our task, we will need an information-purveyor, a place to meet (the design for which is of little importance), and some aids such as books and boards, all of which should serve to purvey information and skills to learners who memorize the information and learn skills for future application.
3. For cost-efficient operation, the supervisor-to-worker and teacher-to-student ratio will be about 1:25. This ratio is of little critical importance to the learning process itself.
4. We all learn in similar ways, so one teaching style will serve all learners quite well.
5. Most will succeed in the system, but we do expect that some will fail. Essentially, that is their problem. It is a tolerable situation, however, as even the school failures can be accommodated in the labor force or supported by the state.

MUCH EDUCATION TODAY IS MONUMENTALLY INEFFECTIVE. ALL TOO OFTEN WE ARE GIVING YOUNG PEOPLE CUT FLOWERS WHEN WE SHOULD BE TEACHING THEM TO GROW THEIR OWN PLANTS.

JOHN W. GARDNER

A DIFFERENT DRUMMER

What has changed or is changing in our assumption base?

1. We can no longer accurately identify the job skills that will be necessary five or more years in the future. Thus, the purveyor-of-content model of the school is changing to a facilitator-of-process model. Rather than focusing on uptake and recitation of limited-life *information* from many unrelated courses, each presented in sequence and following patterns of reason and logic, students now need to learn *strategies and skills* for addressing real-life issues and problems that appear daily, out of sequence, and often in defiance of reason and logic.
2. The role of the classroom professional is changing from teacher, or "sage on the stage," to facilitator, or "guide on the side." The student's resource base is expanding from books and chalk talks to a wider universe of the larger community and, thanks to in-class computers, to a readily accessible worldwide data base.
3. The teacher-to-student ratio, critical in the post–factory-model schooling system, remains critical to learning but, arguably, may become less so as students are encouraged to utilize a community-wide learning base and take responsibility for self-initiated learning.
4. Research is telling us that we each have a personal learning style that is not necessarily the same as the learning style of anyone else, although they all have some similarities (Dunn and Dunn 1992).

5. Finally, we are recognizing that we all began our schooling careers having *already proven ourselves* to be highly successful learners. The concept of failure as a learner, unless introduced in the home or early in the competitive sports environment, is a *school-initiated* concept based on one of the old factory-model assumptions. We cannot afford, in this day and age, to continue to inflict this life-disabling stigma. Children who arrive at the schoolroom door are, with few exceptions, ready, able, and excited to learn. If they do not learn well in the environments we create, we need to create environments that address and honor the ways in which they *do* learn well. Given normal neurologic function, so-called learning disabilities tend to be disabilities inherent in the schooling process itself rather than in the learner. If we are to position ourselves in the monopoly position of "educators to the masses," we need to eliminate failure from the schooling system (Glasser 1969).

THE CHIEF WONDER OF EDUCATION IS THAT IT DOES NOT RUIN EVERYBODY CONCERNED IN IT, TEACHERS AND TAUGHT.

HENRY ADAMS

ASSUMPTION MAKER 2: THE GREAT GOD SCIENCE

During the great renaissance periods in human history, creative, artistic, and intuitive faculties flourished in an atmosphere of support, encouragement, and reward for their expression. We read of people in those periods learning to be accomplished musicians, scientists, and poets, and expressing abilities that we might well consider to be genius or near genius.

We now recognize that cultural factors can either inhibit or enhance the brain's natural ability. Factors present during renaissance periods supported individual pursuits and personal development. Cultural factors present during and following the scientific revolution, however, proved inhibiting to this process. These are some of the assumptions prevalent in the scientific world at that time:

- There is an objective universe that we can measure and know.

- The experimenter can and must be separate from the experiment and must follow prescribed protocol to avoid contamination of the data.

- To facilitate reproducibility of experiments by other scientists, we should rely exclusively on our five senses to observe phenomena, draw conclusions, and interpret results.

- Conclusions of value are derived from reason, logic, and sequential and critical thinking processes. These processes are to prevail in scientific work.

What has changed in the last two hundred years or so?

- It is now accepted that there is no "objective" universe. What we perceive is very much a product of our own neurologic perceptive apparatus. We can never know what is "really out there." Rather, we can only know our own brain's perceptions and representations of physical reality (Zukav 1979).

- It has also been demonstrated that *truly objective* experimentation is not possible. The experimenter affects the experiment; the experiment affects the experimenter (Prigogine 1980).

- The five-sense perception system is indeed appropriate to the science laboratory with its highly select protocol. However, it is highly *inappropriate* in school learning environments when used to the exclusion of more highly developed brain functions, including intuitive and creative thought processes (Ornstein and Sobel 1987).

- The challenges of daily living are far more complex and demanding than the protocols of the science laboratory. Conclusions of value to daily life processes require far more than the limited application of reason, logic, and sequential thought.

Assumption Maker 3: TV, the "Master Conditioner"

TV advertising is, of course, built on *assumptions* and *strategies*. These elements lend themselves successfully to highly effective teaching. Unfortunately, educators have largely ignored them and continue to employ the strategies for learning that have proven less effective (Miller 1990).

What are these assumptions and strategies? If we were to listen in at an advertising agency boardroom meeting, we might hear: "We need to convince people to purchase our products, and the best way to do this is to use *drama, variety,* and *novelty.* We need to strive for *sensory stimulation.* We need to use *humor* and the *unexpected* and at times *bypass the rational, logical, sequential thinking process.* Further, we need to *talk to the personalities* of our viewers." Can we learn from TV advertising copy writers who acknowledge that people respond favorably to the following?

- Being different and individual, but not too different from the crowd

- Being in a preferred-status position, or an imagined one

- Having a sense of personal importance, glamour, worthiness, recognition, and praise

- Having goals that are readily and easily identified

- Having goals that are readily and easily attained or achieved

So far, we do not seem appalled at the prospect of exactly the same kind of education being applied to all the school children from the Atlantic to the Pacific, but there is an uneasiness in the air, a realization that the individual is growing less easy to find; an idea, perhaps, of what standardization might become when the units are not machines, but human beings.

Edith Hamilton

Let's translate this list to classroom-based learning and teaching. In how many classrooms beyond the third grade do we find teachers paying rapt attention to individual personalities; consistently high levels of drama, variety, novelty, humor, and spontaneity; abundant sensory stimulation; and modulated attention to rational, logical thinking? Does this not describe most *preschool learning environments?* Might this account in great part for why learning is rapid, easy, enjoyable, and lasting in early childhood? As we begin to remove these factors from the classroom, learning does indeed become less efficient and we see increasing development of "learning disabilities."

An additional advantage that TV has as a teacher and motivator is that when we sit down to watch a movie or TV show, we typically move into a light-trance state. In this state, we temporarily relax our reason-logic-critical thinking barriers (Lozanov 1978). Stimuli can *bypass* our critical evaluation system, moving *directly* into long-term memory storage.

If our goal as designers of learning environments (which educators are, every working day) is to have school-based learning function as effortlessly and effectively as TV and early childhood learning, it is essential that we operate in environments that are typified by high immediate relevance to the learner; by challenge, fun, novelty, humor, abundant sensory stimulation, attention to creativity and intuition, as well as by reason and logic. We must in these ways tap the part of the brain that learns effortlessly.

IT IS IN FACT NOTHING SHORT OF A MIRACLE THAT THE MODERN METHODS OF INSTRUCTION HAVE NOT YET ENTIRELY STRANGLED THE HOLY CURIOSITY OF INQUIRY ... IT IS A VERY GRAVE MISTAKE TO THINK THAT THE ENJOYMENT OF SEEING AND SEARCHING CAN BE PROMOTED BY MEANS OF COERCION AND A SENSE OF DUTY.

ALBERT EINSTEIN

2

LET'S BRING THAT MODEL UP TO DATE!

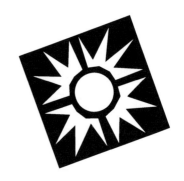

THE ASSUMPTIONS IN BRAIN-BASED LEARNING

Even the brief look we've taken at some of the factors underpinning the assumptions on which much present-day schooling is based can help us recognize that many of the frustrations and problems we face today stem from our cultural past. These "problems" can also be viewed as marvelous opportunities for change. To view them in this way allows us to break away from limited cultural conditions and to design and create learning environments that can elegantly facilitate expanded learning.

WILL THE NEW ASSUMPTIONS PLEASE STAND UP?

Now let's look at important assumptions about how the brain learns best, which are finding application in such diverse fields as biofeedback training, psychoneuroimmunology, business and management, athletic training, and education. These assumptions are that the brain is a natural, talented, and continual learner.

1. Learning is a natural, biologically generated function promoting survival, growth, and development. Learning capacity is enhanced when this inner-drive function is generously supported by stimulation from the learner's external and internal environments (Diamond 1987).
2. Both *externally* and *internally* generated stimuli promote brain activity, resulting in increased neuronal connections or synapses. The more extensive the web of these connections, the greater the brain's capacity in the future to take in information and skills, as well as integrate them and apply them appropriately to life's daily challenges (Diamond 1987).

3. The ultimate capacity of the brain for learning cannot be measured and will never be known, as that capacity increases with use.

4. The brain functions as a *pattern maker, pattern follower,* and *pattern sensor.* From early childhood, the brain establishes patterns based on both verbal and nonverbal messages that come to us from parents and other authority figures. These patterns delineate who we think and feel we are in the world and what levels of success and fulfillment we can expect from our life experiences.

   Having made patterns, the brain uses them as guidelines to drive behavior. These patterns then tend to be acted out in daily experience, generally without our recognizing the connection between them and our actual behavior and experience (Caine and Caine 1991).

   To bring meaning to life experiences, the brain, acting as a pattern sensor, looks for patterns in daily experience that agree with its own internal patterns. New learning is facilitated when the brain can relate newly introduced material to something it already knows (Caine and Caine 1991; Herbert 1985).

   Working directly and consciously with the brain's *pattern-making* function is an example of accessing *expanded* brain function and is at the core of programs for expanded human learning and behavior change, whether these programs be oriented to academic growth, athletic accomplishment, health and well-being or emotional or spiritual growth (Tart 1987).

5. Another example of expanded brain activity is the *Learning Channel* function. When this function is accessed, learning becomes quite effortless and attains a high degree of efficiency (Lozanov 1978; Schuster and Gritton 1986). Young children naturally utilize it, accounting in great part for the ease, efficiency, and effectiveness of learning in early childhood. This faculty tends to be unlearned as we progress through formal schooling and as other cultural factors, such as TV, gain influence. Fortunately, the learning channel function can be reaccessed in the school setting through utilization of brain-friendly teaching methods, opening a door to major breakthroughs in school-based learning and teaching (Hart 1975; Healy 1990; Lozanov 1978).

6. The role of the school-based educator is changing. In crafting optimal learning environments, educators can move from the more stressful role of purveyor of information and skills to the exciting, more relaxed, fulfilling role of facilitator of ongoing, self-initiated and self-researched learning. The terms *teach* and

THE BRAIN IS A SELF-ORGANIZING STRUCTURE. IT ORGANIZES ITS PICTURES OF REALITY TOTALLY WITHIN BRAIN PROCESSES AND PROJECTS THEM IN A 3-D STRUCTURE OUT THERE. THE "OUT THERE" WHICH YOU ARE RESPONDING TO IS A PRODUCT OF THE BRAIN'S OWN MECHANISM. THE "OUT THERE" EXPERIENCE YOU ARE HAVING IS A PROCESS OF THE BRAIN SYSTEM ITSELF. THE BRAIN . . . OPERATES PRIMARILY BY IMAGE FUNCTION.

JOSEPH CHILTON PEARCE

teacher are products of the factory model of schooling. The terms *facilitator, guide, resource advisor,* and *learning environment designer* may be more appropriate to twenty-first century professional roles (Fiske 1991; Martz 1992; Wood 1992).

7. *Intelligence* includes a wide spectrum of abilities and faculties. Research indicates that we have a minimum of seven modes of intelligence and perhaps more than twenty. Traditional Western schooling works with and rewards primarily two modes of intelligence—mathematical-logical and verbal-linguistic. This practice tends to deprive entire generations of their neurologic heritage. Brain-friendly schooling provides environments in which multiple expressions of intelligence can be identified and nurtured (Gardner 1983, 1991).

8. A major brain-friendly approach is to acknowledge, assess, and utilize individual learning styles. Researchers have identified twenty-two factors (most of which are biologically determined) that can powerfully affect our ability to take on and process new learning. Research validates that when students go about their learning in concert with their personal learning style requirements, *all* can be successful learners, regardless of subject matter (Barbe and Swassing 1988; Carbo, Dunn, and Dunn 1986; Dunn and Dunn 1992).

9. Research indicates that the brain functions far more optimally when engaged in challenging (but not threatening) problem-solving thinking. Brain-friendly approaches to schooling engage the brain in higher-order thought processes, utilizing complex *real-life* issues and problems (Fiske 1991; Gardner 1983, 1991; Healy 1987).

10. Emotions are important to the learning process. When one feels threatened or bored, for example, the brain downshifts to a more primitive level of functioning. Under such conditions, teachers can find their charges "unavailable" for higher cortical-level learning. Brain-friendly approaches acknowledge that a safe and calm yet challenging environment—*as perceived by the learner*—is essential for effective learning.

11. The brain recognizes stimuli from both its focused and its peripheral fields. Useful classroom peripherals for enhancing learning include such things as multisensory stimuli, music, taped nature sounds, pleasant aromas, large colored circles on the wall for restful eye focus, and informational posters that are changed weekly (Buzan 1988).

12. Music and sound have important roles in learning. As living beings, we are bio-oscillators (we emit sounds and are affected by sounds at the cellular level). Both internally and externally

WE ARE ALL OUR OWN PYGMALIONS, SPENDING A LIFETIME FASHIONING OURSELVES. IN FASHIONING OURSELVES, FOR BETTER OR FOR WORSE, WE FASHION THE HUMAN RACE AND ITS FUTURE.

I. F. STONE

generated sounds can be effectively used to enhance relaxation and learning. Specially selected music can be utilized to affect many moods, accelerate the learning process, and access human resource states (Campbell 1989; Clynes 1982; Lozanov 1978.).

13. Learning involves both verbal and nonverbal cues and conscious and unconscious processes. Our unexpressed thoughts and body language convey messages of significance at least as great as our words—and perhaps greater. Our *expectations* for students' success/failure, even if not verbalized, can become prophetic.

14. The school's task is to help each student discover and focus on strengths rather than weaknesses, on abilities rather than disabilities. A virtuous function for schooling then, in addition to being a place to learn to manage life challenges, is to be a place to discover personal greatness (Goldberg 1983; Williams 1986).

15. Most of us are more comfortable assessing and judging others' accomplishments than assessing and judging our own, yet part of becoming a self-actualized, successfully functioning human involves the art and comfort of self-assessment. The educational system is in a unique position to develop the art of self-assessment and to reward quality accomplishment as assessed by the learner and then—and only then—as assessed by others (Glasser 1990).

16. School-based education can achieve greater success as a facilitative system by becoming *authentic* and real in the eyes of the learner. This change requires that we move from low-challenge styles of learning, beyond school-generated simulations of life issues, to curricula designed to engage and solve real-life issues and problems, and in the process, to engage high levels of student interest, thinking skills, and involvement (Miller 1990).

Do we have models for brain-friendly settings that can help us to personally validate these assumptions? Can you possibly even validate these new assumptions from your experience? We do in fact have such a model, with which most of us have direct experience. Try the following exercise (see p. 12) and see if you agree.

PHYSICS IS THE STUDY OF STRUCTURES OF CONSCIOUS-NESS. THE STUFF OF THE WORLD . . . IS MIND STUFF.

SIR ARTHUR EDINGTON

Answer each of the questions with either:

PS: for Preschool — **S**: for School — **B**:or both.

1. In which environment is new learning most likely to be *IMMEDIATELY LIFE RELEVANT?*

   —————————

2. Where is *MOTIVATION LEVEL* of the learner likely to be higher?

   —————————

3. Where is *LEARNER-INITIATED LEARNING* most likely to be found?

   —————————

4. Where is passionate *LEARNER INVOLVEMENT* with learning likely to be more in evidence?

   —————————

5. Where is the *LENGTH OF THE LEARNING SESSION* controlled by the learner?

   —————————

6. Where will we find consistently *HIGH EXPECTATIONS FOR SUCCESS?*

   —————————

7. Where will the learner likely find the greatest number of chances to achieve *MASTERY?*

   —————————

8. Where are endless *REPETITIONS* likely to be more acceptable?

   —————————

9. In which environment will we find greater and more consistent personal *OVERT SUPPORT* for each learner?

   —————————

10. In which setting is *IMMEDIACY OF FEEDBACK* greater?

    —————————

11. Where will we find more consistent *APPLICABILITY* of new learning to immediate *LIFE NEEDS?*

    —————————

12. Where is the *SYSTEM OF REWARDS* more varied and readily available?

    —————————

13. Where will learning more likely relate to the learner's *PERSONAL MIND-BODY CYCLES?*

    —————————

14. Which environment encourages the use of *INNER SENSES* as strongly as the five *OUTER SENSES?*

    —————————

15. In which setting is *COOPERATIVE LEARNING* likely to be more highly valued?

    —————————

16. Where will we find *HANDS-ON* activities rather than *LECTURES* to be the primary approach in the learning process?

    —————————

17. Where will we likely find a more consistent expression of *JOY, PLEASURE,* and *PERSONAL ACCOMPLISHMENT* with the daily learning process?

    —————————

LIFE IS FULL OF UNTAPPED SOURCES OF PLEASURE. EDUCATION SHOULD TRAIN US TO DISCOVER AND EXPLOIT THEM.

NORMAN DOUGLAS

Would you agree that early childhood is our period of most efficient, effortless, and joyous learning? Conditions for learning then were quite different from those we experienced as older students (excluding the Steiner/Waldorf system, which more typically incorporates early childhood learning features into primary and secondary grade levels). The questions above serve as a summary of the elements typically observed in preschool settings. All these factors contribute to *brain-friendly learning environments.*

As more of these conditions appear to relate positively to our research-generated assumptions, they underpin brain-friendly and whole-brain learning and teaching models. When we observe models for schools that work worldwide, these conditions prevail in the learning environment. As these conditions are incorporated into school environments, student response is improved in terms of rate of learning, retention of learned skills and information, and in performance (Herzog 1982; Martz 1992; Williams 1986; Wood 1992.)

I AM ENTIRELY CERTAIN THAT TWENTY YEARS FROM NOW WE WILL LOOK BACK AT EDUCATION AS IT IS PRACTICED IN MOST SCHOOLS TODAY AND WONDER THAT WE COULD HAVE TOLERATED ANYTHING SO PRIMITIVE.

JOHN W. GARDNER

PRESCHOOL FACTORS ARE A BEGINNING— THERE IS MORE: "SUCCESS GENERATORS"

How do we take these observations and updated assumptions and use them to create learning places where the bottom line is to have students learn the art of successfully managing their own life issues, feel good about themselves, and find satisfaction and fulfillment in the process? When we observe schools that work, it is evident that there are many factors *in addition* to the preschool factors that bring changes in the desired direction: fuller utilization of expanded brain faculties.

We need to be able to identify these many success-generating factors and to know how to use them to enhance the fuller spectrum of expanded school-based learning. How many of these factors can we introduce into our own classrooms safely, readily, and successfully? Is it possible to gradually and continually add these factors to the classroom curriculum to move closer to our goal with each addition? In the next chapter we briefly explore these success generators.

3

DESIGNING MAGICAL SCHOOLS TO SERVE MAGICAL BRAINS

CREATING SCHOOLING SYSTEMS FOR REALIZING HUMAN POTENTIAL

It's time to pack up our frustrations with getting schools to work effectively and elegantly, hold on to our hats, and take off for the wondrous Land of the Possible. To enhance our adventure, we'll want a model of how the brain learns, and we need to decide what we mean by *learning*. Let's begin by exploring a research-derived model of the brain and of learning.

BRAIN WAVE MODES AND LONG-TERM LEARNING

In traditional classroom settings we strive to have students be fully attentive to what is being presented to them in their immediate physical environment (that is, from the teacher, the chalkboard, and so on). The assumption is that this state of awareness constitutes the best mode for learning. Research is suggesting that this mode is not the best for learning (Caine and Caine 1991; Lozanov 1978; Schuster and Gritton 1986).

It appears that we have a great range and variety of states of awareness, which could serve us richly if we could but access them on call. Psychologist Charles Tart of the University of California at Davis suggests there is a *continuum* of many states of consciousness and emphasizes the importance of being able to access many states at will. To prepare ourselves to ask "How might we create far better environments for learning?" we will look at four major categories of states of awareness, which ideally should be "on call" for each of us at all times. These categories constitute states of awareness that can enable us to perform at levels far beyond our present experience, more closely approximating genius levels of performance. These levels of awareness are Pattern-Maker/High Creativity, Learner, Stress Release (or Relaxation), and Appropriate Action. These correspond to the four channels discussed below.

If we consider radio or TV channels, we know that at each channel, or frequency range, different programs are available. The brain also operates at a range of frequencies. If we were to explain this phenomenon physiologically, we would describe the brain as operating in a normal range of frequencies from 1 to 30+ cycles per second (cps), and we would note that at different frequencies humans can access different capacities, abilities, and talents. The accompanying chart summarizes these channels as they relate to different abilities. (See Caine and Caine 1991; Diamond 1987; Gazzaniga 1985; and Ornstein and Sobel 1987.)

IF THE CHILD IS NOT LEARNING THE WAY YOU ARE TEACHING, THEN YOU MUST TEACH IN THE WAY THE CHILD LEARNS.

RITA DUNN

INTRODUCING CHANNEL 1

When we are fully focused and functioning in the here and now (for example, listening to and watching a teacher's presentation, carefully repairing a broken vase, or attending to an accident victim), we are primarily tuned to our fastest frequency channel (Channel 1). When tuned to this mode, we focus outwardly into the world, guided by our five senses. This is an *output* mode, designed to help us appropriately apply to life everything other parts of the brain have learned. New learning in this mode is limited to "grazing" for bits of information, which go into short-term memory and are quickly forgotten.

"But hold on a minute," I hear you say. "If listening to and watching a presentation while being fully focused outwardly gets us only short-term recall for what we are learning, why do we use this mode for school learning?" Strange as it may seem, sitting up straight and focusing fully on a presentation puts us into a brain frequency better suited for *doing* than *learning.* Under these conditions, we generally require *many repetitions* to get information into long-term memory. For long-term recall or for skill response to become automatic, the desired information must "sink in." Neurologically speaking, this means that information is finally picked up by *another* brain channel operating at a *different* frequency, which we will refer to later as Channel 3.

BRAIN CHANNELS

Brain Frequency Ranges

4 to 7 cps	8 to 12 cps	12 to 15 cps	16 to 30 cps

ACTION CHANNEL

Carries Out Learning ↑

Home of Appropriate Action
- Stressed state
- Outer five senses
- reason, critical thinking
- Acknowledges only external reality

Examples
- Critical analysis of data
- Sit up straight and pay attention

RELAXATION CHANNEL

Home of Transition
- Sees ways to take action

Examples
- Stress Release

LEARNING CHANNEL

Processes New Learning ↑

Home of Real Learner
- Calm state
- Inner senses
- Relaxed mode
- Effortless learning

Examples
- Stress Release
- Inner prime time
- Joy of learning

HIGH CREATIVITY/ PATTERN-MAKER CHANNEL

problem solving lateral thinking
genius self inspiration
creativity invention
artistic talent insight
intuition

Brings Highest Resources ↑

Home of Super Abilities
- Reverie state
- Inner senses
- Available with practice
- Mozart, Tesla, Curie

Examples
- Sleep on a problem
- Creative flashes
- Spiritual inspiration
- Flow state activities

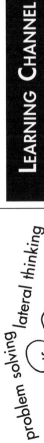

INTRODUCING CHANNEL 2

We display a fascinating ability to take on stress and to release it. In fact, when a subject is connected to an EEG (electroencephalograph) monitor (which displays brain wave patterns), we can pinpoint just when these things happen. We could have our subject imagine a stressful experience, feel the accompanying stress and tension, and then consciously relax and replace the stress-producing

ing thoughts with images of floating on a cloud or basking in the warm sun on a lovely beach. The EEG would show that during the stressful imaginings, brain waves include many waves spiking into the Channel 1 range (15 to 35 cps). As the subject relaxes via calming imagery, the brain wave pattern would change to include more waves in the Channel 3 range (7 to 11 cps). *Between* these ranges we find Channel 2, a very special Stress Release gate of 12 to 14 cycles per second. When we expand our awareness to include Channel 3 waves, we also relax and leave stresses behind. This art is a valuable life-long skill, critical to managing stress and effective learning. Fortunately, educators can learn it readily and teach it to students easily.

LEARNING IS NOT A HUMAN FUNCTION THE SUCCESS OF WHICH REQUIRES EDUCATION THINK-TANKS AND MILLIONS OF DOLLARS OF CURRICULUM DESIGN. FOR EONS, LEARNING HAS BEEN THE BUSINESS OF THE BRAIN. GIVEN STIMULATING AND SUPPORTIVE ENVIRONMENTS, IT IS A PROVEN LEARNER OF GENIUS CAPACITY.

GREGORY BATESON

INTRODUCING CHANNEL 3

This channel, which functions at 7 to 11 cycles per second, appears to be our *learning* channel and is the one that is routinely accessed by preschoolers and in brain-friendly school settings, making learning more efficient, easier, more fun, and often effortless. When we are tuned into Channel 3, learning can occur with up to 300 percent greater efficiency than in Channel 1 (Lozanov 1978; Schuster and Gritton 1986). When we give our students the ability to access Channel 3 at will, we increase their ability to perform and enhance their success in school.

INTRODUCING CHANNEL 4

Channel 4 (4 to 7 cps) is our highest resource state. It is home to our genius self and has enormous, perhaps unlimited, abilities. From this range we access our intuitive thoughts; bursts of creativity; special moments of inspiration and insights; our lateral-thinking, problem-solving prowess; and our inventive talents. Here also are the wellsprings of our artistic talents and faculties. Accessing this high-resource state requires an ability to expand our usual awareness to include an *inner* focus and reverie state in which we are both very relaxed and hyperalert. Many of us reach this state, without recognizing it, when we are in deep thought in a quiet environment.

Wolfgang Amadeus Mozart wrote of his ability to enter a reverie, or dreamlike, state and while there to receive his musical compositions complete, including orchestration. He then brought himself out of his reverie and notated his works. Albert Einstein said that in his mechanism of thought, "certain signs and more-or-less clear images can be voluntarily reproduced and combined" (Hadamard 1945). In his case, these images were frequently visual in nature. Einstein also entered a reverie state for much of his insight work. We read of T. S. Eliot's, Percy Bysshe Shelley's, and William Wordsworth's use of this strategy for creative exploration. We also see evidence of it in biographies of Edison, Rutherford, Curie, and others (Hadamard 1945).

TRUE EDUCATIONAL REFORM WILL ONLY COME ABOUT WHEN WE MAKE OUR EDUCATION APPROPRIATE TO CHILDREN'S INDIVIDUAL GROWTH RATES AND LEVELS OF MENTAL DEVELOPMENT.

DAVID ELKIND

ACCESSING YOUR CREATIVE-INTUITIVE CAPACITY: "INNER PRIME TIME"

Most of us can learn to recognize this special and enormously fruitful reverie state in our own lives. We all seem to have a period of time within every twenty-four-hour period during which new ideas and answers to questions and problems pop into our awareness. You may wish to identify such a time for yourself. It may be while you are in a shower or bath, out walking, or just before you fall asleep or awake. Or perhaps you awake in the middle of the night with new insights and "aha" experiences.

What do these times have in common? These are times when we are in quiet, unstressed settings, with no need for an outward focus. We let our brains coast or go into a free-wheeling mode. At these times our high-level resource channels can communicate with us, bringing their gifts to our conscious awareness.

THE POWER OF THE PATTERN

Let's explore the second major function of Channel 4. Psychologists tell us that much of our daily behavior is "pattern behavior," that is, behavior colored by brain patterns developed in early childhood. How are these patterns or programs created and how do they operate in our lives?

A model of whom we can expect to be in life and what life has in store for us was given to us in our earliest years. Parents and other authority figures gave us many, many verbal and nonverbal cues about what they thought and felt about us. These messages gave us a powerful picture of how lovable or unlovable, bright or stupid, graceful or clumsy we were. The messages may have represented *others' opinions,* but as very young children, we took them to be true. What our brains did with the tens of thousands of messages was to make thousands of patterns consistent with those messages. These patterns then defined our view of who we were and what we could expect from our experiences. The patterns, in other words, served to define in our own eyes our personal worth, image, and expectations.

These messages-turned-brain-patterns operate below our level of awareness and continue to operate throughout life, unless we are trained to *identify* them and know how to *change* them when they do not get us the positive outcomes we want. Until very recent years, we have not considered this ability to be part of what we should learn in school. We now know that this ability can be readily facilitated by most classroom teachers and can help young learners explore the farther reaches of their learning and performance potential—an exciting and beneficial life-long skill.

SOME OF MY BEST IDEAS
COME TO ME IN MY DREAMS.

NORMAN ALEXANDER

BRAIN, GET ME THIS OUTCOME!

How *do* we usually *learn* to do something better, to make long-term changes? Typically we work at it, using practice and repetition, until the brain gets the message that we want a better outcome. If the message we give the brain is loud and clear, it then gets busy to help us achieve that better outcome: it creates a new enabling pattern, which then operates below awareness to drive behavior toward better outcomes.

Although repetition is an established strategy for getting a message to the brain, there is a more efficient and effective way. It is called Positive

Outcome Patterning, and this book will help you develop this skill.

Calling on our expanded powers to bring long-term change is not unfamiliar in our culture. Athletes worldwide use a pattern-creating method to improve their performances. Jack Nicklaus, for example, uses a Positive Outcome Patterning method to improve his golf game and Steffie Graf her tennis game. This approach is used in psychoneuroimmunology, as well as in biofeedback training, in which subjects can learn to control headaches, blood pressure, and other biological functions through non-verbal brain-body interactions. Positive Outcome Patterning and the accessing of our high-resource creative-intuitive capacity are the central skill to which this book is dedicated, as they are at the critical core of all breakthroughs in learning and performance.

It is exciting and affirming for us to recognize that we each have a huge untapped potential or, as Lozanov calls it, "reserve," which when tapped, brings us in touch with outstanding creative and life-changing abilities not usually within the realm of our voluntary control.

It is becoming clear that, given normal neurological functioning, we are all wired for higher levels of learning and performance than most of us ever learn to tap. We lack easy access to the parts of our brain that can realize such potential in daily life. Fortunately, this accessibility *can be learned,* and the school classroom can be the learning environment. Once it is learned, we can push our present limits and begin to enjoy higher levels of personal performance.

4

HOLD ON A MINUTE . . . WHAT DO WE MEAN BY LEARNING?

Here's an interesting question: When you ask a student to *learn* something, what are you asking? From recent brain research, we know there are many answers. Do you want traditional *school-type learning,* that is, taking in information or a skill, storing it in either short- or long-term memory, showing understanding in an out-of-real-life context—classroom demonstration—hoping it will be used appropriately in future real-life situations? We will call this *learning for grades.*

Or are you perhaps requesting learning in the context of more *authentic learning,* that is, taking in information or a skill immediately relevant to the students' interests, storing it in long-term memory, and demonstrating ability to apply it appropriately in real-life situations from which learners get real-life feedback? We will call this *learning for real-life application.* This level is enhanced when the learner knows how to work with the brain's *Learning Channel.*

Or perhaps you would like to request a level of learning represented by the uptake of information and/or skills, storage in long-term memory, demonstration of the ability to apply it in real-life situations, *and* the ability to demonstrate/apply it in real life in six months *better* than you apply it today. This level is enhanced when the learner knows how to work with the brain's *Pattern Maker.*

To achieve this last level of learning, we need to recognize that there are particular brain patterns that *limit* the quality of our present experiences. Then we must be able to *access* the part of the brain that made those patterns, *create a new pattern* designed to allow for more successful future experiences around that issue, know how to *reinforce* the new pattern, and then be sufficiently alert to *note* if and when higher-quality life outcomes are being created by that new pattern.

We will call this *learning for long-term change*. It involves the process of learning how to learn to achieve higher levels of personal performance. This learning process has no limits. Once we can access this type of learning, we can call on it at any time to help us upgrade our personal performance limits in health, sports, academics, and other areas. The more adept we become in its operation, the greater can be our periodic improvement. It can be our magic wand—*the recognition that being able to affect the quality of our future experiences is our grand neurologic heritage.*

TARGETING FOR BRAIN-FRIENDLY SCHOOLING

Now that we've looked at a research-derived model of brain function, as well as some levels of learning, we can focus on our bottom-line question:

Can brain-friendly, classroom-based learning environments more elegantly facilitate students to call on the brain's vast untapped potential for expanded learning and performance, with the ultimate outcome of students being able to effectively manage their personal life issues and to feel happy and fulfilled in the process?

Brain-friendly learning environments incorporate many identifiable factors and well-researched and validated approaches and methods; these factors, methods, and approaches provide us with a base from which curriculum can emerge to establish a schooling process that facilitates learning, problem solving, and personal change of lifelong use and value to the learner.

When identifying the factors that encourage utilization of our fuller brain faculties (brain-friendly learning factors), it might be helpful to use a picture. Imagine a target with a bull's-eye and three concentric rings. The factors in each part of our target play a crucial part in creating the learning environment we're after (see chart, p. 23).

EVEN SLEEPERS ARE WORKERS AND COLLABORATORS IN WHAT GOES ON IN THE UNIVERSE.

HERACLITUS

Before we look briefly at this larger picture of creating more elegant environments for learning, let's note that *learning for grades* is not represented in our target. We recognize that such strategies run contrary

to the natural learning strategies of early childhood and to what brain research tells us about how the brain learns best. Research tells us that this level of learning and teaching tends to lock learners out of their Learning Channel, necessitating many repetitions in order to access longer brain memory.

THE BULL'S-EYE: LEARNING FOR LONG-TERM CHANGE

The bull's-eye of our target involves the process of creating new brain patterns. It also calls into play tapping of our high creativity and intuition faculties. In terms of creating effective learning environments, the bull's-eye highlights the importance of working with both the Pattern-Maker and High Creativity–Intuitive functions of the brain before invoking our rational, logical thought processes.

The following chapters of this book, along with the audiotapes, are dedicated to helping educators become proficient at helping students access and successfully utilize these functions. The story lines in chapters 5, 6, and 7 facilitate relaxation and stress release, opening the door to exercises for improving self-esteem, accelerating the learning process, and breaking new ground in a host of life areas. The exercises encourage learners to make friends with their high resource creative-intuitive and problem-solving capacities. We recognize these capacities when we get insights and inspirations or when we feel "in the flow" (for example, when difficult accomplishments come off beautifully, with little apparent effort on our part).

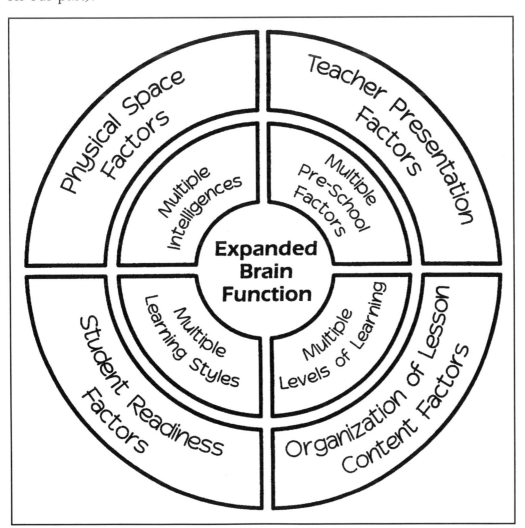

THE BULL'S-EYE

THE SECOND AND THIRD RINGS

Both the second and third rings represent the domain of our learning channel function. By identifying and calling into play important preschool learning factors, students' individual learning styles, and students' multiple intelligences, classroom-based learning can be enhanced. Having already identified important preschool factors, let's now take a look at the other Ring 2 factors.

INDIVIDUAL LEARNING STYLES

This area is one of the more extensively researched in education today. Researchers such as Rita and Kenneth Dunn, Marie Carbo, and the Raymond Swassing–Walter Barbe team have contributed significantly to our understanding that we do not all learn in the same way and that, therefore, one teaching style definitely does NOT fit all.

- Visual
- Auditory
- Tactile/Kinesthetic

As learners, we all have neurologically determined preferred *perception channels*. Some of us learn best by *looking* at what is presented; others need to *hear* instructions; and others prefer to *manipulate* the material to be learned and to *move* around in the process.

One of our tasks is to be aware of, and to help students be aware of, their preferred styles, which represent their perceptual strengths. As educators, we tend to teach in the language and style of our *own* learning strengths and to set up our classrooms in that fashion, which means that we typically force up to 40 percent of our students to use *our* learning-presentation style. Our challenge is to provide opportunities for all modalities, which can be effected by less lecturing and purveying of information and skills and more facilitating students to learn independently and in accord with their personal learning styles. (Dunn and Dunn 1992).

Dunn and Dunn have enumerated some twenty-two factors that temper classroom learning effectiveness. These factors include and go beyond the visual, auditory, and kinesthetic factors, and most appear to be neurologically/biologically based. A few of them are related to social conditioning.

For example, do some students learn and study more effectively when lounging on soft pillows instead of sitting on a hard chair? Or perhaps they learn more effectively while standing? Are some students subject to frequent low blood-sugar levels, making focus-on-task difficult? Is learning improved for some students when they are allowed to work on their difficult learning material later in the day rather than in the morning? Do most people find working under fluorescent lights to be uncomfortable and counterproductive to learning? Do all children work better cooperatively? We recommend that you explore the literature on this subject. Also see the appendix for some examples of useful classroom tactics.

Multiple Intelligences

Harvard University researcher Howard Gardner (1983) postulated that we humans are gifted with not just a single intelligence, forever fixed by genetics, but with many intelligences that can be developed and that can lead us into fuller, richer, or more successful lives. Gardner suggests that there are at least seven intelligences and he identifies these:

verbal-linguistic	bodily-kinesthetic
musical-rhythmic	interpersonal
logical-mathematical	intrapersonal
visual-spatial	

How effective are we in discovering and supporting the individual talent potential of all children who pass through the formal education experience? Does your school define these various intelligences in all students? Does your school develop curricula that nurture and support each student's multifaceted potential via development of these intelligences?

Encouragement to explore and develop our personal intelligence gifts also helps identify brain-friendly learning environments and thus is of critical importance for schools dedicated to tapping fuller brain capacities and fuller human potential.

Additional Pieces to the Brain-Friendly School Puzzle

Many additional factors go into the big picture for creating brain-friendly learning environments. Let's look at four general categories of affective factors that have an impact on classroom-based learning every day. Depending on how these factors are managed, they tend to either inhibit or enhance the brain's ongoing business of learning within the school setting. The categories are

- Physical environment of the classroom
- Readiness of student for classroom-based learning
- Effectiveness of educator's presentation
- Organization of curriculum content

Physical Environment

How does the physical set-up of a classroom inhibit or enhance learning? Do you feel differently inside a vaulted-ceiling cathedral or a large symphony hall than you do in a garage? Have you felt more comfortable in certain rooms and spaces than in others? The answers to these questions might seem obvious to you, but such subtle perceptions are seldom taken into account in the design of schools. Studies on environmental design and learning make it clear that square rooms with flat ceilings, lit by fluorescent bulbs and limited to closed-system air circulation, are indeed *brain-antagonistic* and *inhibit* learning.

Consider the following question, then take a moment to respond in the space that follows: Are there places where you seem to be able to read, study, and learn more effectively than you can in others? Put on your Designer-of-Learning-Environments wizard hat and list a few features of your ideal learning/study environment.

I HAVE COME TO FEEL THAT THE ONLY LEARNING WHICH SIGNIFICANTLY INFLUENCES BEHAVIOR IS SELF-DISCOVERED, SELF-APPROPRIATED LEARNING.

CARL R. ROGERS

Following are nine major features that impact learning via personal and emotional comfort, human physiology and bodily functioning, and our sense of aesthetics. How would these features fit into your own ideal physical setting for learning and into your classroom learning environment?

Room Shape/Configuration

Have you been in rooms that are *other than* square or rectangular? Perhaps in a 6- or 8-sided or circular building? If so, did it feel different to you than the typical room with four 90 degree–angle corners? And how about ceiling/roof configurations? Do you notice a difference in how you feel in a room with a soaring roof than you do in a room with a low ceiling? These elements do have an effect on us.

You are most limited in this category, but you might have fun exploring ways to modify your classroom shape. You could try a Frank Lloyd Wright technique of making walls meet at angles greater or lesser than 90 degrees. For example, place a bookcase or desk across the corner angle, hang a large plant from the ceiling in the corner, and place a poster or tapestry across the corner to give a more open feel. If you and your students like it, try doing something else with other corners.

Focus Areas

Do you sometimes rearrange the furniture in your home? Most of us do. We know that our emotional, creative, and relaxation needs are enhanced in settings that please us and that our needs change. In brain-friendly elementary school classrooms, teachers arrange quiet zones for reading, soft areas for study, areas for listening to tapes, computer areas, and so on. Teachers in middle and high schools allow students to bring cushions, folding deck chairs, and other appropriate seating. (See the video "The Look of Learning Styles" [Learning Style Network, St. John's University, Utopia Pkwy., Jamaica, NY 11439].) It is useful to rezone classrooms periodically (especially crowded ones), with input from the students to acknowledge their needs. This rezoning can enhance the learning value of the classroom space.

Air Quality

The brain consumes about 25 percent of the oxygen taken in by the lungs. An oxygen-rich brain can function effectively; an oxygen-starved brain cannot. Sadly, in our design and equipping of classroom learning spaces, we tend to ignore this fact. We forget that we need cross-ventilation of fresh air. An effective air exhaust system needs to completely replace room air with truly fresh air every few minutes and eliminate the excessive carbon dioxide build-up typical of overcrowded rooms.

The innovative educator can provide a few remedial features. One example is bringing in "air-scrubber" plants, which can perform well as air purifiers (see appendix for recommended indoor plants). You might also consider bringing in several desktop negative-ion generators, which can help somewhat to keep the room filled with seaside-quality air.

Many construction materials used over the years were manufactured using formaldehyde and other materials that in high concentrations can be toxic to humans and at the very least are not conducive to effective brain functioning. These materials can remain in building materials for many years, continually permeating the air. What quality of air do you think you might walk into after your classroom has been locked up tightly for some fifteen to sixteen hours?

We recommend that, weather and windows permitting, you fully air out your room each morning and during the lunch hour. If you have a forced-air system, you might check to see that it begins operation at least thirty minutes before you enter the classroom and encourage the administration to see that the system itself is properly cleaned at regular intervals.

Colors

Our own daily experience reminds us how responsive we are to color. Considering the number of hours teachers and students spend in school, the classroom is a splendid place for experimenting with colors. For example, large colored circles (2 to 3 feet in diameter) placed above eye-level on the walls around the room can be used by students as stress-reduction focal points or eye-rest focus areas, with excellent results.

In the brain-friendly classroom, educators recognize the effects of color on emotions and make use of both fixed and moveable color features. This use includes frequent repainting of classroom walls, perhaps as a student environmental research project, with students and faculty deciding on the colors and design.

AROMAS

Can you recall wonderful aromas from childhood—perhaps freshly brewing coffee or pie just out of the oven or fresh flowers? In brain-friendly classrooms, teachers and students carefully select aromas to anchor their awareness of the classroom as a place of pleasure and delight to the senses. Useful items include whole coffee and vanilla beans, potpourri of herbs and flowers, natural oils such as peppermint and lemon, and so on.

FOOD IN THE CLASSROOM

One of the fifteen assumptions of *traditional* schooling cited by Dunn and Dunn (1992) is that food belongs in the cafeteria, *not* in the classroom. As these researchers also discovered, some children develop low blood-sugar levels more frequently than can be satisfied at school recess and lunch breaks. When blood-sugar levels go down, so does the rate of learning.

Blood sugar levels are likely to swing more frequently and widely in children than in adults. Depending on stage of growth, timing of growth spurts, general metabolic rate, emotional stress, and other factors, children may need their blood sugar "topped-up" every thirty to forty-five minutes if the brain is to be available for learning activities.

In the brain-friendly classroom, naturally sweet real juices are available throughout the day. This availability is most important for students age eleven and younger. Most middle and high schools have lockers where students can keep snack foods, and students should be encouraged to "top up" their energy between classes. This energy boost can effect dramatic results in terms of behavior and focus-on-task.

WATER SOUNDS

How do you feel when you stand near a waterfall, fountain, beach, or in your shower? Flowing, moving water is recognizably beneficial; it makes us feel good. If you can rig up a small flowing-water unit for your classroom, you can further enhance the kinds of feelings that are prerequisites to learning. If moving water is not a practical addition to your classroom, consider an aquarium. Even taped sounds of waves breaking on a beach are effective in reducing stress and encouraging creative thinking.

MUSIC

Sounds affect us in many ways—from being highly supportive and pleasurable to diverting and disturbing. In the brain-friendly classroom, teachers choose musical selections from a wide variety of styles—classical, folk, jazz, environmental, and so on—to help create moods for positive learning experiences. Campbell (1983, 1989), Lozanov (1978), Tomatis (1991), and others have studied the role of music and sound and offer recommendations to teachers who wish to improve the quality of their learning environments. See the appendix for recommendations about using music in the classroom.

Lighting

Have you ever walked into a new supermarket equipped with high-intensity bare-bulb fluorescent lights mounted high up on the ceiling and found yourself squinting and noticing some eye and possibly head discomfort? Contrast that with the soothing lighting at the cosmetic or jewelry sections of department stores, where designers know that incandescent or vapor lamps can increase sales. We tend to use fluorescents because they are cheaper to install and maintain than incandescent lighting.

Tests show that workers under bare fluorescent lights develop a higher rate of skin cancer (malignant melanomas) than people who work outdoors in the direct sunlight all day ("Health Dangers" 1991). Even if fluorescent bulbs are covered with plastic baffles, they are not good for learning places. Why? The rapid-frequency oscillation of the light serves to pace the brain into its faster, Channel 1 Appropriate Action mode and out of its Learning mode and Pattern-Making modes. Thus, fluorescent lights tend to be incompatible with effective learning. In classrooms that use either natural lighting or strategically placed incandescent lighting, there is less stress and hyperactivity and increased relaxation and learning.

Let's Wrap Up

Our focus on the physical space of the classroom can help to remind us that with formal schooling we take the human animal out of its native habitat. The "natural" habitat of childhood is the big wide world with its countless physical, intellectual, and emotional stimuli that encourage development of the brain's network of nerve cells and provide the "preschool factors" (cited earlier) that contribute to rapid learning during early childhood years.

By placing children in a school classroom, we oblige them to adjust to a relatively restrictive setting and then proceed to make increasingly persistent demands on them for high levels of performance. What do we expect when we take a wild animal from its natural, rich habitat and place it in a zoo? Do we expect the new environment to provide the same level of support and challenge to the animal's nervous system as did its native habitat? Do we expect the same high-level displays of the animal's natural talent and potential?

5
READINESS OF STUDENTS FOR CLASSROOM LEARNING

How can we help our students ready themselves for classroom learning and home study? Fortunately, brain research is becoming clearer and more explicit as to student factors that are likely to either inhibit or enhance learning in the school setting. What are these factors? Let's take a closer look.

Research is pointing to the importance of using our brains to solve life challenges, *in a particular sequence:* by first calling into play our High Creativity/Pattern Maker Channel, where our great unconscious problem-solving abilities lie; then, when called upon to learn new facts, by calling into play our Learning Channel; and finally, when ready to act out our solutions, information, and skills, by calling on our Appropriate Action Channel. (Lozanov, for example, has shown that we can learn 500 or more words in a foreign language in a single sitting, effortlessly and with excellent long-term recall, when the Learning Channel is accessed via relaxation, music, and use of directed imagery. Following the learning session, the Actions Channel is called upon to activate the new learnings in real-life simulations in the classroom [Schuster and Gritton 1986]).

In helping students to use their brains more effectively, the brain-based school calls on expanded brain resources, requiring the utilization of both inner and outer senses. The inner senses are used for communication with both the brain's Learning Channel and its Creativity/Pattern-Maker Channel. With our inner senses we can input questions and requests to the brain and be more alert to receiving the brain's responses via insights, inspirations, new ideas, and solutions to life issues. Using inner senses we can also open doors to more effortless learning of new information. Once we have processed creative/intuitive input from the brain and taken on board and synthesized new information that we need, then we call upon the five outer senses to effectively apply all of this, via our Appropriate Action Channel.

ACCESSING THE FULLER RANGE OF BRAIN FUNCTIONS

Learning to access the Learning Channel is best accomplished, for the first few times, with the help of a facilitator. This level of facilitation can be mastered by most teachers in a two-day training workshop or by using the instructions given in this book.

After classroom practice for five-minute periods for a week or two, most students can master the skills of relaxation and of accessing the Learning Channel function. This ability is already "hard wired" into our neurologic system—we naturally cycle in and out of the 7 to 11 cycles per second brain state in every 90-minute period. Thus, we need only to know how to access this state at will and then practice until it becomes second nature, as it was when we were preschoolers.

CREATING BRAIN-FRIENDLY SCHOOL ENVIRONMENTS

FRESH AIR AND BREATHING

In the brain-friendly classroom, students are guided in short breathing exercises prior to learning sessions, preferably in an environment of fresh air.

MOVEMENT

Physical movement is important for comfortable muscle functioning. Understimulated muscles tend to build up body-breakdown products and we get that uncomfortable squirmy or antsy feeling along with the impulse to move. A several-minute aerobic movement and breathing sequence as the first class activity addresses the body's need for periodic movement and can contribute to students being more attentive for class work.

STRESS, EMOTIONS, AND LEARNING

You probably can recall answering a phone or attempting to focus your attention on something and having to shout to someone to "turn down that radio—I can't hear myself THINK!" Under stress, we cannot call on our higher brain faculties, which include the Learning Channel and our High Creativity/Pattern Maker Channel. Our personal stress levels elevate in classrooms by our need to react to distracting noises (telephones, loudspeaker announcements, outside ambient noises). In cases of physical stimulation overload, the brain cycles down to a more primitive level,

ANXIETY IS ALWAYS THE ENEMY OF INTELLIGENCE. THE MINUTE ANXIETY ARISES, INTELLIGENCE CLOSES TO A SEARCH FOR ANYTHING THAT WILL RELIEVE THE ANXIETY.

JOSEPH CHILTON PEARCE

inactivating the higher cortical centers, shutting down learning and creativity functions.

When emotionally over-challenged, the brain also tends to cycle down to its more primitive neurology, its survival mode, resulting in the unavailability of many higher-order cognitive functions. Is your classroom perceived as a safe place for expression of thoughts and feelings? Is it an environment where students are not criticized (verbally or nonverbally) in front of peers or challenged beyond their readiness to respond? Feeling emotionally distressed can rob us of our ability to generate solutions to problems, to be creative, and to relate new learning to what we already know (Wright 1989).

INDIVIDUAL LEARNING STYLES

We all have our ups and downs, some of which relate directly to our personal learning readiness. Dunn and Dunn's (1992) research asks that classroom educators recognize, acknowledge, and honor the personal differences in learning needs among students and allow for expression of indibidual learning needs of all students in our classrooms. Lest this sound daunting, rest assured that their program makes it very easy and effective.

HOW DOES TEACHER EFFECTIVENESS AFFECT CLASSROOM LEARNING?

Teachers have a reputation for being dedicated, warm, caring, bright, intuitive, giving people. Are these not all qualities that should lead consistently to feelings of personal effectiveness and fulfillment as educators? Yet educators complain that teaching is becoming more and more difficult, with overcrowded classrooms, inflexible curricula, and acting-out kids. Any hope?

The good news is that there are approaches that work well. There are highly successful schools, with happy and productive kids, and with educators who feel secure, supported, and effective.

PUTTING TOGETHER PIECES OF THE PUZZLE: MAKING A UNIQUE SCHOOL

When we analyze schools that work, we discover that no two are, or need to be, alike. We can identify, to date, *more than two hundred pieces* to the Brain-Friendly Classroom puzzle. Fortunately, educators can pick and choose as many pieces as will comfortably fit for them and assemble them in their own preferred way. Each added piece helps a classroom become a better environment for learning. We have already introduced the need for calling upon our greater neurologic capacities, via utilization of inner and outer senses and a fuller range of brain function. We will cover this in greater detail in the next chapter.

When we look specifically at teacher effectiveness, we can highlight a few of the key factors that research confirms as important for creating brain-friendly environments for learning.

VERBAL AND NONVERBAL COMMUNICATION

Educators can now access a rich literature on nonverbal communication (Chopra 1991; Dennison 1981). How much of our effective communication is verbal and how much is nonverbal? That's anybody's guess, but some writers suggest that up to 85 percent is nonverbal.

We have already noted that many expectations we have for ourselves and others become prophecies. How many times have you experienced children stopping themselves with an *"I can't!"* expectation? Or have you seen teachers expecting children to be troublemakers or to have difficulty learning—and sure enough, their expectations are fulfilled? We can communicate our negative expectations without speaking a word, and studies indicate that learners do indeed tend to perform to teacher and parent expectations, even if those expectations are not verbally announced.

In the brain-friendly setting, educators and students are aware of the power of thought to influence future experiences. The effective educator uses artful communication at both the verbal and nonverbal levels and is mindful of the power of expectations on the lives of self and others.

AGAIN AND AGAIN STEP BY STEP, INTUITION OPENS THE DOORS THAT LEAD TO MAN'S DESIGNING.

R. BUCKMINSTER FULLER

USING VOICE QUALITY TO OUR TEACHING ADVANTAGE

Voices can be soothing, irritating, calming, exciting, pleasant, or unpleasant. It is a wonder that voice coaching is not included in our professional training. What type of voice do you find relaxing and pleasurable? What voice qualities do you find irritating and ineffective for your own learning purposes? If you were to make a list of the qualities of voice you most preferred in a learning situation, what qualities would you include? Write your ideas here:

Pitch:

Tone:

Volume:

Pacing:

Pauses:

Educators who enjoy working actively with their own development as presenters and facilitators can find satisfaction in exploring the use of their voices in the lower registers, perhaps practice within the context of the *storyteller*. The storyteller is in a marvelous position to encourage utilization of brain faculties. How? As we hear a story, we naturally build images in our minds to bring our own meanings to the words. If we are encouraged by the story, for example, to imagine ourselves being relaxed or successful at spelling or confident when speaking in public, we can imagine ourselves relaxed or spelling successfully or speaking confidently. In this way, we can use the imaginative processes to give our brains messages as to what new patterns we would like them to create and put into operation on our behalf. Telling stories in which the listeners are encouraged to build such positive, enabling self-images can be an effective and enjoyable way to facilitate expanded brain function.

The brain-friendly classroom uses three- to four-minute story lines each day to bring quiet suggestions to relaxed-alert students, then to create mind images of happy outcomes for upcoming events, excellence in performance, and other positive outcomes (Bry 1978; Leuner 1984; Lozanov 1978; Schuster and Gritton 1986; Williams 1986; Zdenek 1987).

IF A CHILD IS TO KEEP ALIVE HIS INBORN SENSE OF WONDER . . . HE NEEDS THE COMPANIONSHIP OF AT LEAST ONE ADULT WHO CAN SHARE IT, REDISCOVERING WITH HIM THE JOY, EXCITEMENT AND MYSTERY OF THE WORLD WE LIVE IN.

RACHEL CARSON

HELPING WITH POSITIVE OUTCOME PATTERNING

Our early-childhood messages and the resulting brain patterns contribute to our daily successes and failures. Some students will be well patterned, for example, to be successful on the playing field but will expect to have a terrible time with history. Some may enter your door with the sense that they can handle anything in school, while some come to you with very low self-esteem and self-expectations.

Until recently, it seemed that even if you were a wonderful teacher, the students who passed through your classroom would be able to apply their school lessons to life only in accordance with their own "I can" or "I can't" brain patterns. Students can learn to apply skills gained in your class better in future years than they can apply them today by knowing how to create new, better-outcome brain patterns. Clearly, a student coming to you with a fearful "I can't" pattern regarding math can greatly benefit from knowing how to build a new mental-emotional "I can" pattern for learning and using math skills. This ability is our "magic wand" (Bandler 1985; Borysenko 1987; Bry 1978; Chopra 1991; Epstein 1989; Ornstein and Sobel 1987; Zdenek 1987; Zukav 1979).

ORGANIZING LESSONS TO IMPROVE THE ENVIRONMENT FOR LEARNING

Let's look at the relationship between how we organize our classroom lessons and the extent to which our students access (or bypass) their high-resource brain capacities. Though there are many factors, let's look at five of the more important:

- ▨ Making the lessons relevant to life
- ▨ Presenting the "big picture" first
- ▨ Accessing intuitive/creative and Learning Channel brain functions before accessing logical/rational faculties
- ▨ Keeping lessons low stress but high challenge
- ▨ Using cooperative learning

MAKING THE LESSONS RELEVANT TO LIFE

This factor stands at the head of the list for creating an effective classroom. Our natural tendency to focus on what is of high personal interest has a neurological basis. Our biological, reticular activating system notices and constantly processes millions of impulses and bits of input from our environment to keep our bodies functioning in the physical world. Only a minuscule number of these impulses ever comes to our *conscious* awareness, as that level of brain awareness function boggles at 7 ± 2 bits of information at a time.

How does this tendency relate to the classroom? If an incoming stimulus is deemed unimportant, irrelevant, or not of interest to *immediate life needs,* the brain prefers to ignore it. If *obliged* to focus higher cortical thought processes on such material, the brain responds by getting bored. Boredom simply announces that the brain, after checking its memory banks, finds the information to be without sufficient *meaning and relevance* to put into long-term memory or to act on immediately. Thus, our understanding of the brain points clearly to *having the learner select and initiate learning* based on high personal interest; such selection is critical to defining a brain-friendly learning environment.

Theme-related learning and *project-based, problem-solving* formats that encourage the learner to identify an area of high personal interest and life relevance open the window for learning. Just how widely it opens and for how long relates to the strength of that interest and relevance.

PUTTING THE BIG PICTURE FIRST

When we put together a jigsaw puzzle, after we spill out the pieces and turn them upright, what is our first step? Fitting the edge pieces together? Perhaps, but even before that don't we always look at the picture of the finished product on the box? Getting the big picture before exploring the details seems to be the way the brain likes to go about its business of learning. Yet in how many courses in your academic career were the *details* presented first: the parts of speech, the parts of the cell, the parts of the equation? And perhaps the big picture was never presented. I recall completing a year course on cellular microbiology without a single instructor pulling the details together to help the class understand the big picture of cell function in the larger organism. What similar experiences do you recall from your own academic experience?

In the effective classroom setting, the mentor helps learners first to grasp the notion of the workings of the entire system. Then, using a deductive approach, students can explore the finer details of that system.

THERE ARE PERHAPS ABOUT ONE HUNDRED BILLION NEURONS, OR NERVE CELLS, IN THE BRAIN, AND IN A SINGLE HUMAN BRAIN THE NUMBER OF POSSIBLE INTERACTIONS BETWEEN THESE CELLS IS GREATER THAN THE NUMBER OF ATOMS IN THE UNIVERSE.

ROBERT ORNSTEIN

Accessing Intuitive/Creative and Learning Channel Brain Functions

When we focus on rational, logical, critical thought, we address a limited scope of brain function. We have no way of estimating the brain's real potential for learning and action, but what is becoming clear is that when our cultural systems (including schooling) isolate our powers of rational thought from daily communication with creative/intuitive brain functions, we can become unfortunately limited both as individuals and as a culture in our ability to call on our fuller brain potential.

Making Lessons Low Stress, High Challenge

Although confirmed research findings have been with us since the work of Swiss researcher and educator Dr. Hans Selye (1956), we can validate in our own lives how difficult it is to concentrate and learn either information or skills when we are experiencing stress levels beyond our biological comfort zone. As discussed earlier, to move into expanded brain states to access our expanded learning modes, we must *relax*. In that process, we expand from the faster 30 to 16 cps range (at which we usually operate in the classroom) to include the intermediate *relaxation mode* of 15 to 12 cps, which is on the way to accessing our *expanded learning mode* of 11 to 7 cps. When we relax sufficiently to include our slow brain waves, less than 12 cps, we also leave stress and tensions behind.

The pioneering work of Dr. Georgi Lozanov points to the importance of true relaxation for expanded learning. In his learning environments and in the classroom settings recommended here, students are instructed in the art of true relaxation, and they use this ability to enable themselves to access their learning channel. This relaxation accounts in great part for the dramatic success of Lozanov's (and similarly designed) methodology for rapid and effortless uptake of new information and superior recall.

TAKING ADVANTAGE OF COOPERATIVE LEARNING

Work at the University of Minnesota by the Johnson brothers has helped us to bring the benefits of working together to classroom education (Johnson and Johnson 1994). Most students prefer cooperative learning at all stages, and it leads to higher quality academic performance.

This brief big picture summary highlights a few of the more important factors, which, depending on how they are managed, can significantly inhibit or generously enhance learning in the classroom. Next we will explore the language of the brain and how we can utilize our intrapersonal intelligence in life-fulfilling ways.

6

FOCUS ON THE BULL'S-EYE

THERE'S HELP ALONG THE YELLOW BRICK ROAD

We have a fascinating tool to help us push out limits and operate at the edges of our expandable personal boundaries. This tool is one of the major language systems used by the below-awareness or "unconscious" brain to communicate with its aware or "conscious" component. The language/tool is *imagery*. We use imagery hundreds of times a day, but *how* we use it can make the difference in life between "blah" and "wow"!

> **Imagine:** If you lived along the Yellow Brick Road in the Land of Oz, where every thought and image that you created would immediately manifest as a life event before your very eyes, how might you use your imagery process differently than you do now? Probably you would direct that imagery rather than allowing it free play all day long. Take a minute to image each of the following and note your internal responses as best you can.
>
> ◎ What is your image for a great vacation setting?
>
> ◎ What image comes to mind for feeling truly relaxed and at peace?
>
> ◎ What images come to you when you feel love for a special person in your life?

When you imagined a superb vacation site, could you begin to note any subtle changes in feelings, in body comfort, in your level of pleasure? When you imaged feeling truly relaxed, did you begin to note any muscle relaxation, inner calmness, serenity?

When you work with the audiocassettes, you will have opportunities to relate thoughts to the direct experience of emotional and physical change. You may note how quickly that change can follow your thoughts/ images. When we choose to harness our imagery processes for positive outcomes by taking a few minutes each day to direct our imagery to what we wish to happen, we are using our neurologic potential to shape and color our future experiences. This is *directed imagery*. It is our challenge as classroom educators to learn the art of appropriately facilitating our or others' imagery in the direction of good, positive outcomes. We can then observe our own experiences and those of our students, noting the body-mind connection that is activated by the brain's language of communication. The aspect of this challenge that can offer us an exciting rationale for integrating directed imagery into our daily classroom program is this: Activation of the brain's imagery powers can *stimulate* and *increase the capacity of the brain to learn.*

YOUR IMAGINATION, YOUR CAPACITY TO FANTASIZE OR PROBE THE FUTURE THROUGH PICTURES IN YOUR MIND'S EYE, IS ONE OF THE GREATEST RESOURCES YOU HAVE AS A HUMAN BEING. YOU CAN LEARN TO ENJOY AND TO CONTROL THE GREAT POWERS OF YOUR IMAGINATION AND FROM THESE INNER RESOURCES YOU CAN OFTEN FORGE A BETTER REALITY.

J. T. SINGER AND E. SWITZER

DID YOU SAY SMARTER?

Let's look more specifically at how we can use the classroom as a place to stimulate the capacity of the brain to learn and perform.

Is being smart a matter of numbers? Since the number of brain cells we have decreases throughout our lives, we might expect to lose some of our learning capacity with age. The good news is that we do NOT need to lose this capacity. How is this possible?

Use it or lose it. Learning capacity depends primarily on communication between nerve cells. Let's use a worldwide telephone network as a metaphor. If our phone network has lines of communication to 150,000 cities, we can readily carry on two-way communication between distant regions. If lines are not established to some regions, we cannot communicate with people there, and we miss out on some of life's possibilities. In the brain, such a network is called a neuron web. If that web is densely developed, all parts of the brain can communicate well with all others.

How does this network grow? As we briefly discussed earlier, the more the brain is stimulated, the more complex the neuron network becomes. These stimulations can come from two sources: the *internal* environment (images, thoughts, feelings) and the *external* environment (experiences in the physical world). Internally generated stimuli are encouraged via experiences such as being read to as a child and being encouraged to develop imaginative and creative thought processes. Externally generated stimuli come from going places and doing things.

The bad news is that many children are coming to the school door doubly disadvantaged. First, they are raised in an environment that did not provide frequent active experiences in the external environment.

Many parents these days are just too busy with their own responsibilities or have a value system that does not include active participation with offspring during formative preschool years. Thus, the development of children's brain capacity suffers and is limited to a fraction of its real potential.

Second, these children are raised in an environment that does not provide a rich set of inner experiences because there is excessive exposure to TV, videos, and movies. These media bring all the components of communication to the viewer, leaving little or no demand on the viewer to bring meaning, creativity, invention, original thought, or problem-solving abilities to the experience. (Video games are an exception in that they do make demands on the cerebral integrative processes.) If and when these higher resource faculties are stimulated, they serve to increase communication between brain cells, contributing in turn to a more complex neuron web and increased capacity for future learning and performance.

WHAT ARE OUR OPTIONS AS CLASSROOM-BASED EDUCATORS?

We could focus more heavily on attempting to make the classroom setting rich in externally generated stimuli, but how successful can we be with such an approach? Can a classroom begin to rival the environment of the outside world? We certainly want to do our best with room decorations, peripherals, and the like but at the same time we must be realistic in not expecting the limited space of a classroom to be a highly effective agent for brain stimulation of the external type.

An option with much greater potential is to focus more heavily on stimulating growth of the brain's neuron network through *internally* generated stimuli. The classroom can be admirably suited to encouraging inner-sense imaging—there are just a few requirements:

> *a comfortable place for bodies to rest*
>
> *a quiet physical setting*
>
> *words used in such a way as to evoke mind-imagery in your students*

Thus, we have what can be a surprisingly fresh and effective approach for facilitating brain growth and capacity to learn, utilizing the classroom environment to stimulate neuron web formation via rich inner experiences. Chapters 7, 8, and 9 provide you with a generous and varied group of directed imagery selections to use in the classroom to help students learn more effectively as well as improve the quality of future experiences. Your own observations of student response to imagery sessions will help you evaluate how well this approach can work for you.

WHAT DO YOU SAY WHEN YOU TALK TO YOUR BRAIN?

PUTTING PEOPLE IN CHARGE OF THEIR SELF-TALK

Our communication access to the brain is via imagery. The brain communicates with us in dream states via images. We communicate with our brains using imagery via our daily mind-chatter, probably without recognizing the possible consequences of this ongoing casual self-talk.

Let's repeat our imaging experiment. Take a minute now to imagine basking on a warm, sandy beach on a glorious day, without a care in the world . . . If you are a good "imagineer," your body will begin very quickly to respond to your imagery with muscle relaxation, release of calming hormones, and many thousand internal responses, leading to a more relaxed state—all due to your seemingly innocent imaging. Powerful stuff. Research has shown that more than 200 hormones can be released by the brain in response to feelings, thoughts, and emotions (Diamond 1987).

We might recognize that thoughts of relaxation can lead to a more relaxed direct experience, but do we consider that the other thousands of images we form each day might also be *precursors* to life experiences? Let's take a closer look at this interesting possibility.

We can acknowledge that the chair on which you sit began as an image/idea in the brain of the builder. Your activities today began with your thought/feeling images about getting out of bed and facing the day. Can you, in fact, think of anything that we consciously do that does not begin with a thought or feeling image?

Thoughts in any form are creative in that they precede and color our intentional creations and actions in the world. We tend to be unaware of this connection, however, when it comes to our daily self-talk. Being aware of this connection and using thought images to seed positive, useful, and happy creations and experiences can be a marvelous personal tool for shaping the quality of our experiences.

In chapter 3 we discussed self-expectations becoming self-fulfilling prophecies. We said that until recently we assumed there was little we could do to help students change long-established thought patterns. Now we know that with patience and good facilitation we can learn to communicate with the Pattern-Maker part of our brains and counter negative-outcome patterning with positive-outcome patterns of our own making. As an educator, you can learn this art for yourself and learn to help your students develop this skill readily and successfully.

We call the art *directed imagery for Positive Outcome Patterning (P.O.P.).* Teaching it involves helping students to become increasingly aware of their daily self-talk, so they can become more self-disciplined

SEVENTY PERCENT OF OUR CHILD POPULATION HAS NEVER DEVELOPED THE ABILITY TO CREATE INTERNAL IMAGES, WHICH WE CALL IMAGINATION. AS A RESULT, THERE IS NO WAY YOU'LL GET THEM FUNCTIONALLY LITERATE, UNTIL THEY BUILD THE CAPACITY FOR THE META-PHORIC, INTERNAL IMAGERY.

JOSEPH CHILTON PEARCE

in dwelling only on images that they are willing to have come true in their lives. Your role as facilitator of directed imagery includes:

1. Introducing your students to the personal benefits that can be derived from positive utilization of self-talk and imaging—and conversely, the hazards of focusing on negative imaging. The brain, being neutral in these matters, tends to go to work to realize both positive and negative images, whatever we hold in a strong focus for the moment.

2. Facilitating student's imagery, during 3- to 5-minute sessions, to facilitate experiences that demonstrate student self-control with stress management, quieting the thought stream, accelerating learning, and expanding performance in many life areas.

3. Instructing your students in procedures for *self-directed imaging* to encourage increasing use of imaging exercises for themselves. In chapter 9 our approach will be to work with self-esteem and self-images by facilitating students to turn their focus from what is wrong in their lives and to focus selectively on what they really want to happen. In this way, students can move from being habituated to outcomes they do not like and feel helpless to change, to a recognition of personal power to help shape and focus life outcomes and creations.

In 3- to 4-minute classroom sessions, both you and students can quickly notice more relaxed bodies, diminished personal stress, and a more cooperative classroom scene. Typically such feedback becomes evident within five or six sessions. Also typically, students will begin to ask for the calming and centering exercises after several weeks of experiencing the results for themselves. We invite you to note for yourself how they work for you as a facilitator, following your experiences with text and tape.

JUMP-STARTING THE IMAGERY PROCESS

STIMULATING IMAGERY DEVELOPMENT AND UTILIZATION

Younger children (under age 10) need little if any instruction for using imagery and delving into their inner senses. They just need permission to do so. We live quite successfully in these dimensions in our preschool years. In Western cultures, traditional schooling and TV tend to pull us out of our natural, highly imaginative, creative inner world by age 10 or so. Indigenous cultures worldwide highly value this inner realm of being and encourage young and old to access it.

As educators, we were ourselves schooled in educational systems that featured and conditioned us in left-brain learning. Therefore, we may not

DEVELOPING AN INNER LIFE IS ONE OF THE MOST CONSTRUCTIVE THINGS A GROWING CHILD CAN DO.

BRUNO BETTLEHEIM

think of ourselves as the best facilitators for bringing balanced, integrative brain activity into the classroom (Gazzaniga 1985; Markova 1992; Gardner 1991; Williams 1986; Edwards 1986; Goldberg 1983).

However, if we can find something inside us that says, "I want to run a learning center where the fuller faculties of the brain are acknowledged and brought into play for everyday living," then we can easily learn to do so. We need to ground our intention by permitting and encouraging learners to reawaken their expanded range of brain faculties and to build curriculum around this focus.

FACILITATING IMAGERY DEVELOPMENT

In inaugurating a new subject or course of learning, we traditionally assume that a content-rich, sequentially ordered lecture/drill system for purveying information and skills is the most appropriate. In facilitation of expanded brain function, the beauty is that all of your charges have already mastered the skills they need, having used them extensively in preschool years. Our task is to remind them of the importance of using the skill and to guide them in a series of short sessions to facilitate reawakening of these natural capacities. They can then advance via curriculum that incorporates short imagery sessions with all new material uptake and activation.

YOU CAN TEACH NEARLY ANYTHING TO ANYONE. START BY PROVIDING FAVORABLE CONDITIONS FOR LEARNING.

ERIC JENSEN

"IMAGINEERING" FOR EVERYONE, BEGINNING WITH THE FACILITATOR

USING DIRECTED IMAGERY IN OUR OWN LIVES

When we observe programs that successfully incorporate expanded or whole brain learning, it is evident that one of the success predictors is *using the skills to teach the skills*. Here is an opportunity for you to explore some of the further reaches of your own neurology.

Audiocassette tape 1, "Meet Your Genius Brain," is for you. It includes a series of easy, effective exercises to help you tune to your higher-resource channels. Once you know how to tune to those states and identify what it feels like to be there, you will be equipped to explore the farther reaches of your own neurologic potential, including high creativity, original thinking, problem solving, accelerated learning, physical health, and sport performance as well as personal life insights.

The tape begins by having you oxygenate the brain through deep breathing. This breathing is followed by warm-ups for stimulating the imaginative processes and a section on creating useful imaginary places. Some of the story lines used on this tape are also used on the student tape so that your experiences can serve in facilitating others using the same material. The tape will help you develop some helpful skills for use on arising and at bedtime. These are followed by advanced work—internally setting goals, constructing positive self-talk, and catching negative-outcome patterns in action and converting them to positive-outcome patterns.

It is always good to keep a journal. You might have your students maintain progress journals to help them increase self-esteem by acknowledging personal growth and successes. If you also keep a journal you will have a chance to observe your own. Record the images you create that feel good and useful to you. Some of your images may remain the same for weeks and months, and others will change. It can be enlightening to look back every month or so at the images you have been using and to note which ones seem to be getting through to your brain to produce some *recognizable results in your experience.* If you study those you can frequently discover patterns or styles of images that can help you create more success-oriented future images.

Affirmations

Imaging works best when we are in a relaxed state, focused within, tuned to the Pattern-Maker channel. To attempt to image when strongly focused on the external environment does not seem to produce the fine results we want. The problem with affirmations, said while focused in our Channel 1 output mode, is that we are not at the same time tuned to our Channel 4 Pattern-Making mode. Thus, simply *saying* affirmations generally proves less effective.

However, when we stop the world for a moment by taking a deep breath and focusing inwardly, we can expand our awareness to include our high-resource Channel 3 and 4 states. If we then *image the outcome we desire,* rather than just say the words, communication with the brain is more effective.

It may well be that the sign of a "renaissance" person is being able to function simultaneously in high-resource Channels 3 and 4 and the lower-resource Channel 1 (frequently identified as a "flow state"). Such a person would be accessing the fuller range of brain faculties and could enjoy the benefits of Channels 3 and 4 and, without delay, act out these benefits in life. We all have such "flow" moments. Our work with higher-resource channels can help you and your students enjoy these marvelous flow states more frequently.

After you spend some time directly experiencing your own expanded brain states, you may wish to explore using directed imagery in the classroom. To get you started in an easy and success-oriented manner, you will want to set the scene for this work. Following is a summary of the details that you need to manage.

SUMMARY OF PROCEDURES

SETTING THE SCENE FOR
DIRECTED IMAGERY IN THE CLASSROOM

These procedures comprise the core features needed to set the stage for directed imagery sessions. As you gain confidence and proficiency as a storyteller, and as you expand your awareness of student needs in the moment, you will recognize how effective you can be as a facilitator of energy levels, moods, and feelings with your students.

A

CALM CLASS
ATMOSPHERE SOUNDS

Mask most extraneous sound.

Select music for relaxation.

Take the phone off the hook.

Place a *quiet* sign on door.

Turn off fluorescent lights.

Use natural lighting or incandescents.

Maintain fresh air circulation if possible.

B

BODY COMFORT
AND RELAXATION

Do an aerobic session of several minutes.

Centering exercise:
With spine as straight as possible, either sit at desk with feet on floor, sit on floor, or lie on back with legs uncrossed. Move as necessary to bring body to maximum comfort.

Take several breaths (diaphragmatic breathing: no rise in chest, just ballooning out of abdomen), then return to normal breathing.

Close eyes or partially close your eyes ("soft eyes") to minimize visual distractions.

Focus within self.

Teacher reads or says relaxation-mode story line.

C

IMAGERY
EXERCISES

For Imagery sessions, start with A and B.

Use warm-up story lines to calm down or bring energy levels up as needed.

Use lesson-specific story line.

Finish with suggestions for returning refreshed, relaxed, confident, and ready for next task (see chapter 5).

Keeping It Fun and Appropriate

Expanded brain function skills are meant to be easy and fun as well as productive. This teaching approach is *not* usual, so if it feels like work, stop and re-evaluate your processes and expectations. If it is enjoyable for you and your students, and your feedback from students, parents, and the administration is positive, then you're on target!

Since this work is quite new to many schooling systems, you may need to communicate with the wider community. We enclose a sample letter to parents (see appendix) that you might wish to put into your own words and send to parents of your students. We want parents not only to feel comfortable with what you are doing, but to support you actively in helping to create a better learning environment for their children.

A Few Suggestions

Gaining Confidence

To gain confidence and proficiency at facilitating imagery skills, you will likely want to use the written story lines in this book until it feels easy and natural to ad lib. With this work, we are attempting to communicate effectively using language specifically styled to encourage students to bring their *own* meaning to our words. As they do so, they form images meaningful to themselves and provide messages that gently suggest to the brain that it get busy achieving outcomes consistent with these images.

Feedback

Fortunately, this work provides its own primary feedback. Educators report that after a week or two of centering-relaxation–stress release exercises, children frequently begin to request the exercises. We know of no more effective procedure for helping a classroom full of people to unburden themselves of stresses brought in from home and other relationships, in a safe and rapid manner.

As your students provide you with positive feedback, you can further develop an ease and flow in your storytelling and eventually ad lib your own story lines. As you continue with these exercises on a daily basis, you may note periods of recognizable improvement in the classroom scene, followed by plateau periods, then additional periods of improvement, and so on. Be gentle and patient with yourself and watch for signs of progress and success as measured by a calmer, more relaxed and cooperative class.

Load your own learning for success by gradually extending your abilities through attuning to times when you sense that the energy in the room could use some raising or perhaps some quieting. If you index the story lines in the book you can flip quickly to one appropriate to your needs.

Becoming proficient at communicating with the Learning Channel and Pattern-Maker brain faculties can offer positive, useful, and surprising outcomes for you and your students. We invite you to enjoy the expansion of student performance as well as your own.

WHAT ELSE

Students will need validation of their own imagery process and content from time to time. They may need you to affirm them in a nonjudgmental manner. Use such phrases as

> *"Your images are just right and perfect for you."*
> *"We each have our own image language. Go with your own."*
> *"That's just fine."*
> *"Take what you get and work with it."*

What do the images mean? As with dream interpretation, imagery provides a fascinating opportunity for students to discover what their inner images mean for them in their daily lives. It is helpful to view these "mind movies" as our *personal language symbols.*

It also helps to remind students that when images arise that the students do not immediately understand, they should go back inside and ask for meaning and clarification. This process is important as it helps them to rely on their own authority. It is an empowering exercise to ask a question of personal importance and then to reach inside for the answer rather than always to look to others for answers. Your classroom can be an excellent training ground for attuning to one's process of "inner knowing."

BUILDING STORY LINES

Story lines are of two types in terms of what they say: *content rich* and *process rich*. For example, we might invite learners to imagine lying on a sunny beach, with the delicious, smiling sun gently warming them all over so that they can feel comfortable and very relaxed, and then proceed to guide them through a relaxation exercise, muscle group by muscle group. This is a content-rich story line.

After several such relaxation sessions, when students have created a favorite relaxation site in their imaginations, we can use process-rich imagery. We can simply suggest, for example, that students take several deep breaths, easily take themselves to their favorite relaxation place, and in a short time feel completely comfortable and relaxed. In this case, there is no specific content suggested, just suggestions for their own inner processes.

We recommend this progression from high to low content as most of us (especially younger children), when being introduced to directed imagery, need specific content suggestions to help build personal images. At some point, each participant will have her or his own sets of images,

THERE ARE CHILDREN PLAYING IN THE STREETS WHO COULD SOLVE SOME OF MY TOP PROBLEMS IN PHYSICS, BECAUSE THEY HAVE MODES OF SENSORY PERCEPTION THAT I LOST LONG AGO.

J. ROBERT OPPENHEIMER

filled with personal and unique content, and once they rehearse a few times the last thing our students will want is for us to be continually injecting specific content into their imagery. You will therefore gradually use less and less content, leaving more and more to the students.

We thus use content-rich stories when learners of any age are in the early stages of creating inner places and helpers that will be available to serve them on many levels of learning and doing. The "places" and "helpers" we create are metaphors. They are the content of our images, which, when called up from a relaxed-alert state, or alpha state, can serve as messages from one part of the brain to another, calling on expanded brain faculties to enhance successful learning and action in the world.

Your function as facilitator is to set the scene, create a quiet and comfortable environment, offer suggestions, and expect success. Students will do the real work of creating images meaningful to them, thereby sending messages to their own brains regarding what they want their brains to get busy accomplishing.

TO LOOK AT THE WORLD FROM A NEW PERSPECTIVE IS TO DISCOVER A WORLD OF NEW POSSIBILITIES.

STANISLAV GROF

BUILDING CUES FOR THE LEARNING BRAIN

There is an advantage to identifying favorite story lines and using them frequently. Do you remember in early childhood asking a parent to read you the same story for the umpteenth time? As soon as that story was begun, perhaps you took yourself to the Land of Imagery, to the Land of the Possible, to other realms that were as real as anything experienced in the world of the five senses.

As you gain confidence facilitating students, you can find yourself adapting additional cues, both verbal and nonverbal, to signal "it's time for a quick imagery session." You might wish to experiment using particular voice inflections or volume, by using gestures, by walking to one special place in the room, and by changing environmental features such as dimming room lighting and playing quiet background music. You may find it interesting to stack verbal and nonverbal cues to subtly create just the right setting for imaging.

INTRODUCING STUDENTS TO EXPANDED BRAIN FUNCTIONS

Here are a few thoughts that you might wish to put into your own words and share with your students, as part of your introduction to directed imagery.

You might think that tales of magicians and magic wands are just kid's stuff, but magic wands can be more real than you ever thought possible. The world's best athletes now train with a "magic wand" that they use to transform themselves from excellent performers into SUPER athletes and medal winners. What is that wonderful bit of magic, and where can you get some for yourself?

That magic wand is a 3 ¹/₂-pound super-computer, capable of enormous feats and greater accomplishments than you have ever imagined. YOU have been carrying one around on your shoulders for years. Yours can learn up to 500 vocabulary words in a single learning session and recall them months and years later without any effort at all.

Yours carries out tens of thousands of precise and enormously complex electrochemical processes every hour to keep your body alive, and it does so with a precision that boggles your usual awareness even to TRY to imagine it! Your computerlike brain HEALS your body of invasions and injuries of all sorts. Every cell knows precisely what to do. Given special instructions by you, it may even speed up that healing process.

It stores every single event of your life in its amazing memory banks. It can energize your body with tremendous power and strength in an emergency situation. It can learn to speak many languages fluently and quickly. You could get to know three or four languages just as readily as you learned one if you were better prepared to use your brain's real potential for learning.

If you can learn how to speak your brain's language, it can help you improve your performance in sports, movement and dance, acting, academic performance, and many other areas. You already have, right now, all the brain ability you will ever need to be a super learner and super performer. All you need to learn is how to get that tremendous ability working better for you.

MORE SUGGESTIONS FOR STUDENTS

Images are the way one part of your brain communicates with another part. The brain runs your body and your learning. If you can learn to use the brain's language of images to give your brain the instruction you want it to have, it can serve in many wonderful ways to help you become a better learner and to use your learning for a better life.

THE BEST LEARNING STATE IS IN BETWEEN BOREDOM AND ANXIETY—A RELAXED, HAPPY CONCENTRATION . . . NOT A FORCED ONE.

ERIC JENSEN

◎ *When learning how to do imagery work, we'll do things, such as finding a comfortable position for your body, using special breathing exercises, and following a few easy instructions. When you're good at this, you'll be able to use images to communicate with your brain at any time, whatever you are doing.*

◎ *You are in charge of what you think and image. If you have any uncomfortable thoughts or images, stop and open your eyes if you need to. Then close your eyes or partially close them again and imagine a very pleasant thought or image.*

◉ *There are no right or wrong images or experiences. Some of your experiences will be totally new to you and most will delight you. Take what you get (unless it is not what you want, and then CHANGE IT to suit your needs).*

◉ *Your images will likely be different from others' images. Work with your own as they are your personal bits of communication with your brain. These exercises are not competitive but a way for you to become good at communicating with your powerful brain for purposes that can prove very useful to you.*

◉ *Allow images to come to you effortlessly. Just ask for an image and see what happens. No "trying" here! Trying, in fact, gets in the way.*

Of the hundreds of images we form each day, some are picture images, some are feeling images, some are self-talk images. People image in a variety of ways, and all ways are valuable. We do not usually consider these images to be important or special or even to be precursors to future experiences. But they can be all of these, and you'll get an opportunity to experience them yourself.

We can easily recognize that the chair we sit on began as a thought image in the brain of the designer. Our activities today began with our thoughts and feelings about getting out of bed to face the day. Can you think of anything in which we participate that does not begin with a thought, feeling, or image in our heads? (Allow time for students to think about this and for a short discussion if needed.)

THE "SURE ENOUGH" PRINCIPLE

How many times have you expected, say, to have a good time at a party and you did? Or maybe you expected to have a lousy time and, sure enough, you did. We call this the "sure enough" principle, and it reminds us that our expectations (one kind of thought image) tend to get acted out in our lives. Physics research even suggests that thoughts are indeed creative acts that influence how we perceive our experiences every day—good or bad, happy or sad, successful or not. How we use our thoughts is important because just as thoughts and chairs are connected, so are thoughts and experiences. The problem is that we are seldom aware of the connection between our thoughts and our experiences and so are not able to use thought images to shape our future experiences and make them happier and more useful for us.

Over the next few weeks, we will be exploring some exercises that can help you recognize that connection between your thoughts and your experiences. The exercises will be fun and can be very useful to you, to help you relax and let go of tensions, to do better in athletics, get better grades in school, and feel better about yourself.

7

USING BRAINS FOR HAPPY GAINS

Our mission as school-based educators can include safely and constructively helping students explore the vast potential and amazing possibilities of our neurologic heritage. Our bottom line is to use that potential to better meet our daily life challenges with ease and elegance.

In the rest of the book, we will be working with the core of our Target Model, which involves learning to communicate with fuller brain function via the tool of directed imagery. The general procedure is easy. You and your learners lead off with a series of thoughts and feelings and explore the results. We imagine a quiet scene and note how our bodies respond. We imagine ourselves increasing the range of body movement and observe the fascinating result. We mentally rehearse our athletic performance and note that we can get better results. We imagine being successful in the school play or on an exam or when giving a speech or writing a story, and we have the opportunity to note more positive outcomes.

We can thus observe the link between thoughts as creative, causal impetus and experience as the effect of that causal impetus. The classroom environment can serve as a safe "game board" of life, so that we might observe how we can improve our life movements using thoughts and feelings to influence which scene or square we land on in 30 seconds or tomorrow or next week.

INTERMISSION

At this point, please review the audiocassette regarding suggestions and instructions for facilitating others into expanded brain states.

The next chapters provide you with a variety of graduated story-line choices to use with your students. We recommend that you begin with story lines for *relaxation* and *stress release* and use one or two imagery exercises each day for two weeks, requesting feedback from your students following each exercise. This procedure will help you evaluate how directed imagery works for you.

SUMMARY OF PROCEDURES

1. *Oxygenate body* with several minutes of physical exercises such as those recommended in the appendix.
2. Have students *find comfortable positions* for their bodies, sitting or lying down.
3. *Oxygenate brain* with several full, diaphragmatic breaths.
4. Create an environment for *focusing attention inward* using a story line from this book or one of your own creation.
5. *Use either content or process* imagery or some of both.
6. *Return students' focus* to the room, inviting them to bring back good feelings and recommending that they take a full breath just before opening their eyes.

TEACHER SUGGESTIONS

As mentioned, one predictor of success with directed imagery is to *use the skills* in the process of facilitating them. Therefore this is an opportunity for you to *image yourself* as relaxed and your students as pleased with the outcomes of the exercise. These images need not have any particular faces on them or even on any particular activity going on. Just go for the feeling you want as an outcome. Want to feel good, confident, and successful? Then image those feelings, knowing that you are in your classroom with your students. No additional content is necessary.

Note student responses over time and draw your own conclusions as to how directed imagery can contribute to making your classroom a brain-friendly and effective environment for learning. You might review the Letter to Parents in the appendix and consider distributing copies to parents before imagery and relaxation and stress-management work.

In the exercises offered here, a series of dots indicate a pause of fifteen seconds, and the word *pause* indicates a thirty-second pause.

GETTING STARTED WITH STUDENTS

THE RELAXATION GATE

This activity formally introduces your students to the notion of tension versus relaxation and offers them a level of experience that many (we hope all) will welcome. Following are sample instructions that you can put into your own words for your students.

ONE OF THE GREATEST MIRACLES OF THE BRAIN IS HOW WE REMEMBER SOUNDS, VOCAL TEXTURES, AND UNIQUE MELODIES. THE VARIATIONS ARE SUBTLE, BUT THEY MAKE A SUBSTANTIAL IMPRINT IN OUR MEMORY.

DON CAMPBELL

Today we will learn a skill that you can use every day of your life . . . It's called the RELAXATION GATE. You know that a gate is something to pass through that gets you into new territory. Our gate today is a very useful one. On one side of the gate are stress, worry, and tension. On the other side are relaxation, calmness, and feelings of well-being.

Let's talk about this gate and how it works, then we will do some exercises and have some experiences of how to pass through the gate, from tension and stress to relaxation and calmness, whenever you feel the need for it.

Learning how to relax deeply and get rid of stress is something like learning how to tune a TV set or a radio. What does that mean? Well, our brains operate on several stations or channels, as does a radio or TV. We'll call our brain channels Channels 1, 2, 3, and 4. There is a gate between each channel and the next, and what you need to know is how to open those gates so that you can work with information from several channels at one time.

WE ARE NOT FATED PRODUCTS OF OUR ENVIRONMENT. OUR CIRCUMSTANCES ARE THE PRODUCTS OF OUR OWN INTERNAL PROCESSES.

JOSEPH CHILTON PEARCE

The channel you are most familiar with we'll call Channel 1. As you fully awaken in the morning, your brain automatically tunes you in primarily to Channel 1. It's your "being awake and doing things" channel. It gets you out of bed, washed, dressed, fed, and off to school and keeps you going all day long until you put your head on the pillow again at night. When tuned to Channel 1 you are operating through your 5 outer senses—sight, touch, taste,

smell, and hearing. This channel is very handy. Its keeps you from falling off your chair and allows you to move your body around in the world . . . very handy, indeed.

There is one minor problem, however, with this channel. It is also the home of tension, stresses, worry, and anxious feelings, which can give us stomachaches, sore muscles, headaches, high blood pressure, ulcers, and lots of other ills, all of which can be very uncomfortable for us.

Some stress is okay, but many of us pick up too much distress, worry, and anxious feelings at times and wish we could get rid of them. The good news is that recent brain research tells us that we CAN learn to get rid of stress, but that doing so depends on whether or not we know how to tune in to Channel 2 while staying in touch with Channel 1 (so that we don't fall off our chairs). Channel 2 is known as the RELAXATION CHANNEL. As we learn to access it, our stresses and tensions can evaporate like magic.

You can learn to tune into Channel 2 and you can experience real relaxation and inner calm no matter what is going on around you. We'll practice this tuning and then talk about what we did so that you'll know how to let go of your stresses and worries whenever you need to.

BREATHING FOR RELAXATION, LETTING GO OF STRESS, AND FOCUSING ATTENTION (AGES 7 AND OLDER)

When stresses are on the mind, the body is squirmy, and thoughts are chattering away in the head, classroom learning is hopeless. This short exercise starts students off on developing the art of relaxing the body, quieting thought chatter, and tuning out distractions. These skills are critical to expanded brain function and focusing of attention on schoolwork.

STUDENT INSTRUCTION

Let's learn a very useful skill. We can use our breath to calm our body and to let go of stresses and tensions that are bothering us. The way we let go is to take a full, slow breath and then let it out. Simple . . . but there is a skill to it. How do we take a "full" breath? How do we get the lungs really filled with air? You might think we do this by expanding the chest, but there is an even better way: expand the tummy [abdomen, navel, or whatever terminology best suits the age group]. Remember that the lungs need room to expand and the most room is made available not by expanding the chest but by expanding the diaphragm, which is below the lungs. So, we expand the tummy [here you will likely need to draw a picture on the board showing how the lungs can inflate as the diaphragm expands]. So, place your hand over your tummy. As you breathe in, allow your tummy to expand so that your hand is raised up a bit. Then as you let the air out, your hand moves down again. Breathe in slowly and note how your hand rises and falls, rises and falls as you breathe. Good.

SECOND STAGE

Instruct your students to hold the inhaled breath to the count of four, breathe out and hold the exhaled breath to the count of four. We do this round four times:

Breathe in deeply and slowly so you can feel your hand rising. Hold your breath to a count of 4, let it out slowly, and hold the exhalation for a count of 4. Now do this—breathe in and hold it, breathe out and hold it . . . Now twice more on your own . . . Good.

Now just let your body breathe you . . . and be aware of the air coming in . . . and the air going out . . . breathing in . . . breathing out . . . breathing in . . . breathing out . . .

I CLOSE MY EYES WHEN I WANT TO SEE.

PAUL GAMARIN

BREATHING TO FEEL GOOD (AGES 7 AND OLDER)

This exercise has students focus on breathing, adding light and warmth and good feelings.

STUDENT INSTRUCTION

Close your eyes and let your awareness go inside . . . Note how your body feels . . . Does it need to move just a bit to get more comfortable?

Now take a deep, full breath the way we learned a moment ago: hold it for a count of 4, then exhale and hold the exhaled breath for a count of 4. Breathe in and hold it . . . breathe out and hold it . . . Breathe in, and this time let it go with a sigh . . . so you can hear the air going out of your lungs . . . Once more now breathe in deeply and hold it . . . now breathe out so you can hear yourself breathing out . . . Good. Now just let your body breathe and notice how nice and relaxed you can begin to feel . . . how easy and calm you can start to feel . . .

Now imagine that way deep inside of you is a tiny light . . . It is very bright . . . It is your own special light and it can help you feel relaxed, calm, and warm . . . and as you watch it now, it can begin to grow larger. With each breath, see it expand and begin to fill up your body with a beautiful, sunshiny glow . . . and the wonderful warm glow fills your body and can find any place that might need some special attention so it can feel better. Where is that place? . . . Where can the warmth of the light help you to feel better? And perhaps you can even sense that as you fill with a bright warm light, you can feel better all over . . . warm . . . and calm . . . filled with your own special light that lets you feel good all over . . .

Good . . . And now, gently allow that imagery to fade . . . just let it go . . . because you can bring it to you whenever you like . . . and now we are going to refocus into the room . . . gradually . . . taking your time . . . to wiggle your fingers and toes and take a slow deep breath just before you let your eyes flutter open . . .

IMAGINATION IS MORE
IMPORTANT THAN KNOWLEDGE.

ALBERT EINSTEIN

WARM-UP EXERCISES TO GET IMAGES FLOWING

TEACHER SUGGESTIONS

We suggest that students send their overtrained judgmental faculty "out to lunch" for the duration of the exercises. Doing so will offer a necessary focus when students are learning to allow images to flow readily and in an undistorted fashion. And, as we have already discussed, the unimpeded flow of imagery is critical to calling on expanded brain states.

When reading these story lines, allow about 5 seconds or so between phrases or questions for the brain to present images to the aware self. Use a soft, slow, low-pitched conversational voice, and you'll do just fine. You might wish to generate student discussion of their experiences and ask for feedback on your presentation style.

Forget about punctuation and syntax in the wording of the story lines. What is important is the flow of ideas. Ellipses between phrases remind you to pause. We frequently use run-on sentences and other violations of grammar when working with expanded brain states to facilitate those states of awareness.

WE ARE WHAT WE THINK. ALL THAT WE ARE ARISES WITH OUR THOUGHTS. WITH OUR THOUGHTS WE CREATE THE WORLD.

THE DHAMMAPADA

ICE CREAM CONE

Go inside now, and imagine that you are standing in front of a chalkboard or whiteboard with a colored marker in your hand . . . Now reach out to the board and draw a nice circle on it . . . Good . . . Now step back and note how the circle looks to you . . . What color is your circle? . . .

Now imagine an ice cream cone appearing inside that circle. . . . It has your favorite flavors . . . Perhaps you can see the colors of the ice cream and the cone . . . Now reach into the circle and take the ice cream cone into your hand. (Pause.) It is a very warm day and the ice cream is beginning to melt . . . just a bit . . . so you'll want to lick it all around . . . tasting the creamy flavor . . . and perhaps feeling the coolness on your tongue and throat . . . And it can be fun to take a bite of the ice cream and get a mouthful . . . Can you feel the coolness on your teeth and tongue? . . . How delicious can that be? . . . Now it's time to let that image fade . . . just let it disappear, . . . and as I count slowly from five to one, you can get ready to open your eyes: 5 . . . 4 . . . 3 . . . 2 . . . 1.

VACATION

Go inside now and imagine that you are standing in front of a chalkboard with a marker in your hand. Reach out now and draw a very large circle on the board . . . As you watch that circle you may note that you can allow a beautiful scene to appear . . . a scene of a place that you'd love to go on your vacation . . . the most perfect vacation place for you that you can imagine . . . a place where the weather is always just the way you like it to be each day . . . and you get to play your favorite sports and games . . . and do just what you like to do. (Pause.) So let's take a look around now . . . What do you see way off in the distance? . . . What are the shapes and colors you see? . . . And now look in closer . . . and what do you see? (Pause.) And now look just around you . . . What might you like to reach out and touch? . . . And are there pleasant aromas? . . . And are other people there with you? Can you recognize any of them? . . . And on this vacation you get to have the foods you love . . . Perhaps you can imagine what they are . . . Can you imagine your favorite breakfast foods?

(Pause.) And what would you like for dinner? . . . And since there is so much to do here that you love to do, in just a moment you'll take two minutes of clock time—which can seem like hours of inner time—to enjoy your vacation . . . doing just what you want to do . . . and seeing how much you can enjoy it . . . So let's get ready to do that . . . now (Pause. After 2 minutes, gently begin speaking again.) Good . . . I hope you had a wonderful time on your vacation. We'll take them frequently . . . so you can return to this place or maybe to a different one next time . . . that's up to you . . . You may want to remember what you did here so that you can share it with a friend in a minute or two . . . Now refocus yourself into the classroom, wiggle your fingers and toes, and after 30 seconds or so, take a deep breath and let your eyes flutter open.

THINKING IN PICTURES
PRECEDES THINKING IN WORDS.

IMMANUEL KANT

Have students turn to the persons next to them and take a minute or so each to share what they enjoyed most from their vacation experience. This oral sharing helps to fix the images in memory and builds enthusiasm for the ability to call up positive and helpful images at will.

IMAGE YOUR PARTNER (AGES 10 TO ADULT; YOUNGER IS OKAY BUT THERE MAY BE GIGGLING)

This is a fun exercise for practice in allowing images to flow unimpeded by critical assessment. Pause between the questions so that each segment takes about two minutes.

STUDENT INSTRUCTION

In this exercise we will have some fun with our creative talents and you will learn something important about your creative, inventive self. The objective of the exercise is for you to note how new thoughts and ideas come to you from your very talented and creative brain.

You will need to sit opposite someone in class whom you do NOT know very well, and imagine what your partner would be like if he or she were something else, such as a cloud or a mountain. There will be no speaking during the exercise, and you'll probably feel more comfortable with your eyes closed, but that's up to you. When you have had several opportunities to have fun allowing images to come to you, you can talk to your partner and share what you imagined.

Now choose someone in the room you do not know very well and sit facing that person.

Good . . . Now take a few seconds to go inside and center yourself . . . just be still inside your own head . . . be aware of breathing out and breathing in.

In a moment, I will ask you some questions. When I do, you will probably notice images that come into your awareness. That will be good

. . . just let that happen. If no images come, that's okay, too . . . This is an exercise where you don't want to try to do anything . . . just let it happen. When images do come to you, take what you get. Don't toss any out or try to change them . . . just remember whatever comes to you.

Okay, I'm going to invite you now to imagine your partner (slight pause) as a tree. What does that tree look like? . . . What does the trunk look like? . . . Take a good look at how its roots are growing in the soil. And what are its branches like? . . . Where does the tree live? Is it by itself or with others? . . . Does anything live in the tree? . . . What feelings do you get about this tree? . . . If the tree had feelings, what might it tell you about itself and how it lives? (Pause.)

And in just a moment, you can simply let the image of the tree fade, because it's time to image your partner as something different . . . This time, you are invited to image your partner as a (slight pause) bird. What does the bird look like? . . . What is its size? . . . And are its feathers all one color or several colors? . . . Is the bird standing still or in motion? . . . Where does it live? Is it by itself or with others? . . . What is it doing? What feelings do you get about this bird? If the bird had feelings, what might it tell you about itself?

Good . . . in just a moment we can let the image of the bird fade because I'm going to invite you next to image your partner as a (slight pause) body of water . . . it could be a river or a stream or a lake or an ocean . . . whatever comes immediately to you. How does that water feel to you? . . . Can you sense part of its shoreline? . . . What do you see there? . . . Can you pick up something of interest along the shoreline? . . . Does the water make sounds? . . . Can you tell if anything lives in the water? . . . Is the water home to any creatures? . . . If the water had feelings, what might it say to you?

After completing the imaging, partners can take about five minutes each to share their images. You might also have some discussion about what students think the purpose of the exercise was, how it felt to do the exercise, and whether or not some of their images felt particularly good or "right" to the partner.

With regard to this last item—images that occur during this exercise can on occasion prove to be intuitive "hits" that identify how another person feels about him- or herself. Thus, even though our purpose is to help stimulate free flow of images and to encourage students to notice how they perceive imaginatively (via pictures, feeling states, or mind chatter), other intriguing and positive spin-offs sometimes surface.

You can use subjects in addition to the ones we have suggested, for example, a plant, the wind, a clown, a work of art, a cloud, a mountain, and so on.

With older students and adults we generally add a fourth subject: *If you were to imagine your partner ten years in the future, doing just what*

he or she really loves to do in life, what images might come effortlessly to you now? This subject can be a fascinating one for further opening to what the inner senses can bring us. When we focus our attention in this way, the brain can work on the intuitive level to produce information that is not knowable via the five senses only. We have all had hunches that have been accurate. For example, most of us have had the experience of knowing who was on the other end of the phone before we answered it. Usually our extensive intuitive abilities lie dormant, but imaging gives us the opportunity to develop these abilities.

During the fourth exercise in this series, some students will identify their partners' "secret" interests quite accurately. This short exercise can thus be a fun and safe way to introduce students to the play of intuition. You can use this Awareness Series on its own or follow up with an expressive exercise such as writing, dancing, or painting.

MAY THE WORLD IN SOME STRANGE SENSE, BE "BROUGHT" INTO BEING BY THE PARTICIPATION OF THOSE WHO PARTICIPATE? THE VITAL ACT IS THE ACT OF PARTICIPATION. "PARTICIPATOR" IS THE INCONTROVERTIBLE NEW CONCEPT GIVEN BY QUANTUM MECHANICS. IT STRIKES DOWN THE TERM "OBSERVER" OF CLASSICAL THEORY.

J. A. WHEELER

ALICE STORY LINE (AGES 8 TO ADULT, WITH SOME MODIFICATIONS)

Begin with the opening ritual: comfortable body, straight spine, eyes closed, three deep breaths, go inside . . .

And as you find that perfect place, begin to feel yourself able to relax . . . breathing in a favorite color . . . filling up with it . . . feeling yourself become even more comfortable . . . easy now . . . and relaxing . . . finding just that right place so you can feel waves of comfort flow over your body with each breath . . . breathing in that color . . . and as you breathe out . . . let it flow like a wave . . . from your head down to your feet . . . a wave of good feeling . . . and you might wonder what it feels like to be perfectly relaxed . . . all over . . . now . . . and beginning to feel quite heavy . . . delightfully heavy now . . . your body becoming very comfortably heavy . . . and so relaxed . . . and getting even heavier now . . . and how strange it can feel and how nice it can feel to find yourself becoming very heavy . . . and very comfortable at the same time . . . as if your body were made of a very heavy material . . . feeling so heavy and so comfortable . . . because now that heaviness can begin to leave you . . . slowly at first . . . then more quickly . . . as your body becomes lighter . . . becoming lighter and lighter now . . . until you are back to your normal weight . . . and how nice that can feel too . . . as you continue to become even lighter now . . . very, very light . . . almost like a feather . . . as if you could lift right up so easily . . . and so fascinating just how light you can feel . . . and easy to do . . . and all the weight going out of your body, until you can feel almost weightless . . . so that you could even float up into the air . . . and you might even feel that you could rise up from where you are now . . . just a little . . . and then settle down again . . . very comfortably and slowly . . . and you can feel great pleasure in this . . .

discovering your normal weight once again . . . and it can be so very pleasant to become aware of your own body . . . and its marvelous ability to be comfortable . . . and be very aware of your body now . . . and observe to your surprise that you are growing smaller . . . shrinking now . . . and getting smaller still . . . as Alice did in the story Alice in Wonderland *. . . when she drank from the bottle labeled "drink me" . . . and you can just keep getting smaller . . . down to four feet tall . . . and to three feet tall . . . and down to two feet . . . and one foot . . . growing even smaller now . . . very, very tiny . . . about six inches tall . . . so easily, and confidently . . . And how does a chair look to you from there? . . . and a table? . . . And how does that look . . . And you can do this easily and with great pleasure . . . because now you are starting to grow in the opposite direction . . . getting larger once again . . . up to one foot . . . two feet, three, four feet . . . and growing still more quickly on up to your normal size . . . and not stopping there but keeping right on growing . . . larger . . . and larger . . . up to six feet tall and then seven feet tall . . . eight feet and feeling very, very big . . . like a giant . . . with a giant's strength and a giant's energy . . . feeling very good and strong . . . and powerful now . . . and notice how much you can enjoy that feeling . . . because now you are beginning to slowly and easily return to your normal size again . . . and normal body awareness . . . and feeling good . . . and very talented to be able to do these things . . . and in a moment I will count from five to one . . . and you can count silently along with me . . . taking a deep breath when we reach two . . . five . . . four . . . three . . . two . . . now take a very deep breath . . . one . . . now gently let your eyes flutter open . . . and smile at someone . . .*

You may wish to add experiences to the Alice script to help students increase their repertoire of imaging abilities. These are good warm-ups for creative expression such as creative writing, graphic arts, and drama, as well as for problem-solving activities.

Here is an example of an additional Alice image:

. . . and you can notice how your body outlines are becoming blurred . . . the distinction between your body and the surrounding spaces is becoming indistinct . . . and noticing how very easy and natural and comfortable this state can be as you can become one with the surrounding environment while still maintaining your own identity . . . or . . .

Finding yourself in a forest . . . a very peaceful place in nature . . . and now your body can take on a greater density . . . noticing your body becoming dense . . . like wood . . . like a young tree (pause) body changing into that of a young tree . . . full of vigor and growth . . . and very supple and healthy . . . gently swaying . . .

GENERAL RELAXATION EXERCISES (AGES 5-8)

Okay, now take a deep breath . . . hold it . . . let it go . . . Now find a comfortable place for your body . . . wiggle around a bit until you find it . . . Good . . . Now take another deep breath . . . fill up your tummy . . . as much as you can . . . hold it . . . then let it go . . . push all the air out . . . one more deep breath . . . let it out easy . . . good.

Pick out a place on the ceiling and just look at it. Keep on looking at it until the rest of the room seems to disappear and it's easy to do . . . while you can just let the rest of the room fade away . . . good. Now slowly let your eyes close part way or completely and feel the warmth and pleasure of closing your eyes . . . while you tell your muscles to relax and tell your hands and arms to let go and just sink into the floor and wiggle them a few times until they get the idea . . . Now do the same with your legs and feet and wiggle them around a little . . . roll them from side to side . . . and tell them to let go and relax. And wiggle your jaw around, from side to side, really fast . . . and take a deep breath, and blow the air out through your whistle-lips . . . just loud enough so that you can hear the air rushing out.

Now tell your thoughts to quiet down . . . and watch a few clouds go by in your mind . . . now some more clouds because it's easy to feel so good, so relaxed . . . Think of something really fun that you like to do . . . now wiggle your toes . . . now wiggle your fingers and hands . . . and get ready to open your eyes.

ONE NEVER LEARNS TO UNDERSTAND TRULY ANYTHING BUT WHAT ONE LOVES.

GOETHE

GENERAL RELAXATION EXERCISES (AGES 7-16)

Begin with general relaxation introduction, or tense-relax technique for quieting the body.

Now let's take a trip inside our minds. Close your eyes, and I'll talk to you for a while. And as I talk to you, you can relax even more . . . feeling really good lying on the floor . . . safe and calm . . . expecting to learn how to do something nice today that will be of real help to you, to relax even more. Something inside you knows very well how you can get to your center right away and . . . easily and . . . there are so many ways that you will discover . . .

Because today we'll learn a new one. You'll like it because it's easy and it works . . . and as you listen to my voice, let it take you deeper inside you, so you can feel that good feeling of letting go and letting the floor support you . . . knowing you are safe here . . . and as you feel better and very calm, imagine that there is a lake . . . very calm and still now and

If the school sends out children with a desire for knowledge and some idea of how to acquire and use it, it will have done its work.

Sir Richard Livingstone

. . . right in the center of your body . . . a tiny lake that is very still and . . . a peaceful clear lake with fresh, still water . . . and now as you feel calm, just like this lake, drop a pebble into the center of the lake, and feel the gentle ripples spreading slowly and smoothly from the center . . . out into your body . . . with ripples spreading out into your chest and legs and arms and hands and neck and face and head . . . and let the ripples calm even more . . . smoothing your body, bringing relaxing feelings from the center of your body out to your toes and fingers and head . . . feeling good. (Pause.) And you can get that feeling again anytime . . . to find your center any time . . . whenever you like . . . by just closing your eyes, taking a deep breath, and going back to that lake inside you . . . and dropping a pebble into that calm lake, and feeling it spread calm all over your body . . . because you can do it any time and it works.

GENERAL RELAXATION EXERCISES (ALL AGES)

The current demand for stress management books and courses confirms that knowing how to relax is one of the most important skills we can learn. The following activity helps dissolve muscle tension by the alternate tensing and relaxing of muscle groups. It is initially a fairly long exercise but, once learned, can be shortened to 15 to 20 seconds.

This type of exercise is great before taking exams, participating in sports activities, speaking before a group—or a thousand other occasions. Have students lie on the floor, preferably on blankets or mats or other soft surfaces. If the floor would be hard on your back it will be hard on theirs, so you try it first.

We are going to learn how to really relax . . . from head to toe. The first several times we do this exercise, it will take you a while to work your way through your body, but as we get to know how to do it, we'll be able to relax in a matter of seconds. Let's begin by lying on the floor on your backs and not touching anyone else. Move around a bit until you get as comfortable as you can. Now, close your eyes and think of your hands . . . Make tight fists with your hands . . . tight as you can. (Pause several seconds.) Good, now relax your hands . . . and feel the warm tingling feeling you get as your muscles say, "Ahh, we can relax now." . . . Now bend your arms and make a muscle, making your arms very tense and tight. (Pause several seconds.) Now relax and let your arms go limp on the floor beside you. Good, now shrug your shoulders . . . pushing them up to your ears . . . and hold them there for a few seconds, tightly. Okay, now let them go and feel how good that feels.

Keeping your eyes closed, open your mouth wide, until you can feel your face muscles stretch . . . like in a yawn . . . and close your mouth

. . . Now press your tongue hard up against the roof of your mouth . . . and really feel the pressure. Good, now let it go and feel how nice it feels to relax your tongue. Okay, now wrinkle up your nose and make some funny faces . . . hold it. (Pause for several seconds.) Now let it go, and imagine your face becoming very smooth and soft. Now tighten your stomach muscles. (Pause for several seconds.) Now relax them . . . just let them become soft and easy . . . Now tense all the muscles of your legs . . . very stiff and tense. Hold them. (Pause for several seconds.) Good. Now relax your legs . . . and feel how warm and good they feel, almost like sinking into the floor . . . Now curl your toes really tight . . . hold them in that position . . . then relax.

Now . . . take three slow, deep breaths, and each time blow the air out so that you can hear yourself exhale. Breathe in warm light, and breathe out all of your tightness . . . Again, breathe in warm light, and breathe out all of your tightness . . . now . . .

Good . . . let yourself feel the difference between being tight and tense and being relaxed.

We'll do this exercise again a few times, and very soon you'll be able to relax quickly and very, very fully . . .

You might finish this exercise by suggesting to the students that they imagine themselves being lightly brushed, like with a very soft brush, all over the face and body.

RAPID RELAXATION (ALL AGES)

This exercise is the short version of the last one, to be used after several practices with the longer version. This exercise can be done while lying, sitting, or standing. It is a good one for all ages to prepare for any tension-producing activity.

Close your eyes. Now take in a breath . . . not quite a full one. Hold the breath and tense every muscle in your body. Hold the position . . . now let go . . . Take in another breath . . . not quite a full one . . . and again, tense all the muscles of your body for a few seconds . . . then let it all go and say to yourself "relax." . . . Really let go when you tell yourself to relax . . .

Good. Now take a full breath . . . and do not tense your body . . . just hold your breath . . . Now, let the breath out forcefully and as you do say silently to yourself "relax." . . . When you feel like relaxing, just take a deep breath, hold it for a few seconds, and as you softly let it out, say "relax" to yourself, and let the breath go. You can do this anytime and anyplace and no one will know that you are doing it. Now practice doing it a few times—deep breath, hold it, then release it as you tell yourself to relax.

LET'S FLOAT ON A CLOUD (AGES 6-11)

This is a short exercise to enhance further the sense of true relaxation and release of stress and anxieties. It is best used in conjunction with a more formal relaxation exercise. This one is also good to prepare for imaginative, creative work.

Begin by lying on the floor, on a comfortable surface, on the back, and wiggling around a bit to find the most comfortable position for your body. (Pause for about ten seconds.)

Look at the ceiling, and choose a spot to look at. Just let your eyes focus on that spot, until the rest of the room fades away . . . all there is is just that spot. Good, now take a very deep breath, and as you let it out, let your eyes gently close . . . and feel how warm and relaxed they are. As you relax your mind, and just let it float along, imagine lying outside on a lovely warm day . . . sun shining warmly on you . . . feeling good all over. Now imagine the sky . . . and watch the clouds float slowly by. See the shapes the clouds take . . . animals . . . birds. (Pause for ten seconds.)

Now find a place in your own body that feels very relaxed . . . the most relaxed place in your body right now . . . and imagine that part of you is like a cloud . . . warm and nice, and let that part of your body become a warm cloud . . . and then let that cloud get larger and spread to other parts of you . . . into your chest and down into your legs and feet . . . and all over . . . until all of you is floating along inside . . . this beautiful, warm cloud . . . and very peaceful and totally relaxed . . . all the while feeling happy and joyous . . . and your own cloud protects you from anything outside of you that you want to keep away from . . . because you know and can let your cloud be one of your centering places.

And now it's time to come back to the people around you . . . so take your time to keep the good feelings you have, and count yourself back from 5 to 1 . . . and when you reach 1, open your eyes, feeling good and happy, peaceful and alert.

BODY STRETCHING (AGES 5-10)

Human bodies function most efficiently and comfortably with alternating periods of movement and quiet. These cycles in adults are approximately in 90-minute intervals; children experience 15- to 45-minute cycles. Stress and tension increase when we ignore these cycles.

As we learn more about how the brain learns, we recognize how essential it is to acknowledge the needs of bodies and minds. Certain movements are helpful in permitting the body to release pent-up tensions.

Have children begin by simply walking around the room, being attentive to their own spaces. Stop them after a minute or two and have them put sufficient space between themselves for outstretched arms to

OUR BRAIN IS LIKE A
MANSION. THE PROBLEM
IS THAT WE ONLY LIVE
IN THE LOBBY.

MARION DIAMOND

64

swing without hitting another person. Have them begin walking again, maintaining that space.

As you walk, raise your arms up, stretching as high as you can on each step . . . feeling yourself stretching from toes to finger tips. (Pause 1 minute.) Lower arms. And now take slow giant steps, stretching your legs. (Pause 1 minute.) And now bend forward and walk like a chimpanzee, with your fingers nearly touching the floor. (Pause 1 minute.) Now stop walking, and raise your arms up over your head. Now bend gently from side to side like a tree in the wind . . . feeling the stretch all the way down the side of your body. Now the other way . . . hands high, and bend, feeling the stretch. Good. Now pretend that you are picking fruit from a tree above you . . . reaching first with one hand, then with the other. Each time, feel a real stretch down the side of your body. Good . . . now stand with your feet spread apart. Put both hands up high over your head and put hands together. Now bend forward as though you were chopping wood . . . then up, and chop wood again. Good . . . now lie down on your back . . . pull knees up to chest and rock back and forth a few times. Okay . . . now stand up again . . . and put your arms out to the side, and swing your upper body, twist, twist . . . Now slow that down . . . and slower until your arms come down to your sides.

Follow this exercise with lying quietly on the back and perhaps doing an eye-palming exercise.

Make up your own series using exercises that feel good to you. Check with your students after each series about how it felt to them to do the exercises—which ones felt very good, okay, and not so good to them. Then modify your series to suit your students.

Finding Our Center While Standing (all ages)

Wouldn't it be nice if we could always remain centered, always balanced, always feeling fine? This exercise helps us find that center place within.

Find a place in the room to stand, where it feels comfortable. Let your eyes close and let your body relax. Let your eyes relax . . . easy . . . letting your ears take over for now. Bend your knees just a bit so that they are not locked. Relax your shoulders, chest, stomach. (Pause.) Now let your body rock gently from side to side . . . shift your weight from one side to the other. Keep rocking, but slower and slower, until you find for yourself a perfect balance . . . feeling just right. (Pause until all are still.) And now, rock very gently forward and back . . . easy now . . . and let yourself find the place where you stand straight and tall . . . with almost no effort . . . your weight balanced evenly on your heels and toes. (Pause until all are still again.) Good. Now imagine that you have a body inside that no one else can see. Let it rock from side to side until it feels centered . . . Good . . . now let it rock back and forth until it is centered perfectly inside you.

Now let yourself feel what it is like to be perfectly balanced. Imagine a tiny, bright ball of light inside you, and imagine that you move that light down to a spot . . . just below your navel. Put your hands over that area and imagine that the light is inside you right there, shining very brightly.

Now gently open your eyes, and start to walk very slowly around the room . . . imagining that you are moving from that point of light . . . very slowly walk, feeling tall and centered, moving from that ball of light . . . That's your center point. Whenever you need to feel centered while standing up, just do this exercise . . . rock a bit from side to side, back and forth, until it feels just right . . . then put that tiny ball of light into your moving center . . . and start to move, letting that ball of light lead you. You'll feel very confident and sure of yourself when you move from your center point.

GREAT IDEAS ORIGINATE
IN THE MUSCLES.

THOMAS EDISON

This centering exercise has multiple applications. Here are some suggestions for using it with students:

- Use to calm students before lessons requiring intense concentration
- Use to prepare students for any competitive event
- Have students take their pulse before and after centering exercises (this can be related to a science or health lesson)
- Parents can use it at bedtime when kids are all wound up and too excited to go to bed
- Use it to help kids improve their posture: Have them imagine a string emerging from the top of the head and a balloon floating above, holding the head in perfect position; kids put their hands over their moving centers and walk slowly around the room.
- Use before any creative activity, to help students slow their brain waves and thus better access their creative abilities
- Use when standing before the class to give a report

Now can you think of a few applications? . . .

CREATIVE WALKING (AGES 5-10)

Intensive cognitive work can be enhanced by preceding it with five minutes of focused-body work. To keep students focused, slow the motion of an otherwise commonplace activity.

Call the group together in an expanded circle with arm room between students. Direct them to do the following in slow motion, giving 2 minutes (or however long it feels right for your group) to each example: march, swim, climb, walk against a strong wind, ski, skate.

If you have appropriate movement music, use it. You might finish up with the "move from your center" exercise. Students can move in their own manners and in whatever directions they choose, avoiding contacting others. Or you can have students contact others, perhaps with just the backs of their hands or forearms, and then both move together. This can build to three or four or more moving together.

Examples of additional indoor and outdoor exercises include the following:

- Move in a close space with eyes closed. Move slowly to try to avoid bumping into another person.

- Walk briskly, arms swinging, in wide outdoor areas, and focus on enjoyment of swinging the arms.

- Imagine a string tied to the top of the head and held up by a balloon. Walk straight and tall as if fully supported by the pull of the balloon.

- Teach students how to juggle, alone or with another person (this can be an excellent centering exercise).

- Choose partners. Blindfold one partner and have the other lead the blindfolded partner around obstacles.

TRULY PRODUCTIVE THINKING IN WHATEVER AREA OF COGNITION TAKES PLACE IN THE REALM OF IMAGERY.

RUDOLF ARNHEIM

ADDITIONAL CENTERING EXERCISES

There are many exercises you can use for centering. For example, you can have your students sit in a circle with a candle in the center. (A thick candle is more effective than a thin one.) Then give these instructions:

Move around a bit until you find that really comfortable sitting position. Let yourself sway sideways and forward and back just a little bit, with eyes closed . . . just to find that perfect place for your body . . . Good. Now take three slow, deep breaths, filling with air, then breathing it all out again . . . breathe in light, and breathe out any tightness or worrying thoughts. (Use metaphor of blowing negative thoughts into a balloon, a cloud, and so on. Pause for about fifteen seconds while students breathe in light and blow out negativity.)

Now let's look at the candle for a while . . . looking at the flame and feeling very relaxed . . . watching how the flames move in the air, and letting any hurts or negative thoughts go to the flame and burn off. See how soft the flame is, and your body can be that soft. So slowly the flame moves and dances, like your thoughts, so slow and easy. (Have children watch the flame for several minutes, while you occasionally use what the flame is doing as a metaphor for how they can be quiet.)

Now close your eyes and watch the images inside your head. (Pause for a minute.) Now, feeling very relaxed and rested, slowly open your eyes. Do some easy stretches.

You can successfully use a variety of objects for centering. Examples include the following:

- **Classroom aquarium.** A proven mind calmer. The larger the better. Best mounted in a wall at a standing child's eye level.

- **Classroom waterfall.** Bring in a garden waterfall sculpture with a water pump and get it working in the classroom. It can be magic for some children.

- **Sound.** Borrow a white noise generator from the science department and turn it on during times of stress (as a storm builds up, prior to the start of rain, for example).

- **Baroque music.** Play largo or adagio movements from baroque and romantic period music. The beat per second paces the brain into a slower frequency alpha range of 7 to 11 cycles per second.

- **Classical music**. Introduce the class to selected classical and quiet jazz music compositions, chosen for their calming rhythms and sonorities. Also check out some of the new age or environmental music for similar benefits.

NONE IS SO GREAT THAT
HE NEEDS NO HELP, AND
NONE IS SO SMALL THAT
HE CANNOT GIVE IT.

KING SOLOMON

HINTS FOR FACILITATING THE EXERCISES

1. Begin with a general approach, using a simple exercise. Later create specific exercises for specific needs.
2. Give instructions in a conversational, peaceful voice, not unusually slow or affected. (Tell yourself to relax and note your voice patterns.)
3. Use the written models at first until you feel ready to ad lib.
4. Consider that what you are doing is simply giving students permission to do what they normally do every day. You are not passing on knowledge, facts, or even feeling states. This awareness might help you relax into the process and thus be even more effective.
5. We call what we are doing *calming, centering,* or *focusing* as these are neutral and readily understood terms. Other acceptable terms are *balancing, tuning in, tuning, self-talk,* and *quieting.* You can discover other terms that will be acceptable to both students and their parents.

Centering must really be experienced to be understood. Students have described it as "feeling right inside," "feeling good," "being balanced," "quiet inside," "no thoughts," "lighting up inside," "peaceful." Centering is best done lying down on the floor or sitting cross-legged, unless your classroom chairs are exceptionally comfortable.

WHAT IF . . . ?

. . . students giggle and disturb?

Expect it to happen. Some students will feel uneasy and embarrassed about closing (or partially closing) their eyes or doing some of the exercises simply because they are new and different and unexpected classroom behavior. If your style is to acknowledge behavior, it can be reassuring to uneasy students for you to explain this new classroom style to them, advising confidently that they will have fun and learn more easily.

Most students will welcome the relaxed feelings and soon be asking you for imagery time, but it may take some students several weeks to adjust their conditioned expectations. If children continue to disturb the class, they can be given the choice to listen or do quiet work elsewhere in the room.

WHAT IF . . . ?

. . . a student does not want to close the eyes?

It is easier to image when sensory stimulation is reduced. Outer images tend to overwhelm inner imagery, but it is perfectly possible to learn to image with the eyes open. If some learners do not wish to close their eyes, they may keep them open. With experience using the exercises, most students will feel safe and comfortable with their eyes closed. If closing the eyes is not acceptable, then looking down at the floor with half-closed eyes can be just as effective.

WHAT IF . . . ?

. . . some students fall asleep during imagery time?

This is natural and okay. Many students will from time to time lose your voice directions during imagery sessions. Our Master Bio-computer System is "on duty" 24 hours a day regardless of whether we are awake or asleep. Because this Master System is constantly alert to cues from the physical environment, it is also alert to your voice and will awaken sleeping students as you suggest they return their awareness to the room. On rare occasions a touch on the shoulder will be needed to realert a student. For the repeated sleeper or snorer you might suggest he or she sit up with the back well supported during imagery time.

WHAT IF . . . ?

. . . a student has trouble imaging?

We all create inner images, many hundred times a day. Most people—but not all—can hold a visual image. Some people form *word* images (talking to themselves inside their heads) or *feeling* images. Many will also be able to *taste* and *smell* in their inner imagery. The objective is for students to develop as rich and extensive a repertoire of inner sensations as possible. It is important to first explain that we do not all image or imagine using the same inner senses. You might further explain that you will use the term *image* or *imagine* rather than *visualize* . . . and it is up to the students to note how they form the image . . . via a picture, feeling, or words. Multisensory imagery can be more highly effective than calling on just one sense. Therefore, you might suggest in an exercise "allow an image of an _____ to come effortlessly to your awareness now . . . and note how it feels, and how it looks, and what it sounds like . . . (or tastes and smells like)." Both you and the students will frequently be pleasantly surprised with the richness of the inner images experienced with such open-ended suggestion.

WHAT IF . . . ?

. . . a student does not want to participate?

Imagery work is best when the critical left brain says, "This is okay for me to do." Accept the learner's choice not to participate, but insist on respect for other learners' rights to have an uninterrupted experience. The student can be given quiet work to do that will not disturb others.

8

USING THE MAGIC OF YOUR MIND

CREATING RELAXING IMAGES (AGES 7-ADULT)

This exercise encourages multisensory awareness, including sight (with colors), the sense of touch, and inner feelings of well-being. It also encourages self-permission to feel good, which can be stabilizing and healing for any of us.

Begin with a short body-movement exercise. Follow with the usual sequence of comfortable body, straight spine, closed eyes, three deep breaths, going inside.

Imagine that you are standing in a beautiful garden on a warm sunny day, feeling good. The sunlight showers down on you . . . Can you imagine yourself standing in a shower of beautiful sunlight . . . feeling the gentle warmth that can feel calming . . . as it pours over you from head to foot? . . . Can you see it and feel it as it takes on wonderful colors? (Pause.) Washing you with light (pause) moving over your head and through your brain . . . cleaning it and making it bright? . . . Let the light fill your face so that it glows. (Pause.) And now imagine the light moving down your shoulders and back and chest and arms . . . and pouring off your fingertips . . . as it fills your whole upper body with good feelings. (Pause.) And now feel and watch the light as it moves down over your hips and legs and feet and pours off your toes . . . as your lower body lights up. (Pause.) How good can it feel to you as every part of you is filled with a warm, loving light? (Pause.)

Whenever you feel finished with the exercise, wiggle your fingers and toes and bring yourself back into the room . . . slowly . . . and take a deep breath before opening your eyes.

QUIETING THE CHATTERING MONKEY-MIND (AGES 6-12)

Begin with comfortable body, straight spine, eyes closed, 3 deep breaths, awareness focused inwardly.

Good . . . I invite you to imagine now a bright beam of light coming out of your forehead . . . Watch that beam and note whether it is white or colored. (Pause.) How strong a beam is it? Can you see it? . . . Can you feel it? (Pause.) Can you now make the beam brighter . . . brighter still? (Pause.) And now can you spread it out to cover an area as large as the entire classroom? (Pause.) Now can you focus it into a narrow beam about as wide as a pencil? . . . Like a laser beam . . . very powerful . . . sending it right out into space so it could even bounce off the moon? (Pause.) Good . . . now can you use your beam of light to carry some good feelings to someone who is very special to you? Whom might that person be? (Pause.) You might want to see that person all lit up with the light of your beam, feeling very good . . . perhaps with a smile on his or her face . . . And now you might want to allow yourself to feel good about that too . . . being able to use your light for good. (Pause.) Let's do something special now and have your beam of light come back inside your head. Can you turn it around so that it lights you . . . all over . . . with a warm and loving light . . . so that you can feel good all over? (Pause.) How good can that feel? (Pause.) And whenever you feel that you are finished with the exercise . . . take your time . . . get ready to return your focus to the room . . . move your fingers and toes and, after about 30 seconds, take a deep breath and open your eyes.

NOTHING HAPPENS UNLESS FIRST A DREAM.

CARL SANDBURG

CONE OF LIGHT (AGES 6-12)

Here is another short exercise that uses light imagery. It is good for calming, centering, and energizing. Begin with the standard relaxation ritual.

Get yourself very comfortable now. Find that best place for your body . . . where you can feel comfortable . . . and moving around just a bit until you find that place . . . good . . . Now take in a deep breath and slowly let it out . . . and don't close your eyes until you have taken in a second deep breath . . . and then softly exhale . . . easily . . . and another breath . . . and softly exhale it . . . How relaxing that can feel . . . and now I invite you to imagine that you are standing in a beautiful place (pause) and you can be aware of your place becoming more bright . . . as if the lights were being turned up . . . and brighter still . . . and this light is warm and feels very good . . . a gentle, loving light. (Pause.) Can you tell, is the light white or does it have color? (Pause.) And perhaps you can notice that your hands and feet can begin to feel warmer . . . from the warmth of the light (pause) and even perhaps begin to tingle nicely as the light fills your hands and feet . . . and soon that warm and tingling feeling can begin to spread to your legs and arms . . . so that you can feel them glowing with light . . . as the light continues to spread into your chest and hips . . . so it can warm your body . . . because it is spreading up into your head as well . . . so your whole body is filled with a comfortable glow . . . and you can feel good all over . . . and how does that feel? (Pause.) And now let's take a minute of clock time, which can be all the inner time you need to imagine how good you can feel when filled with a very special warm and loving light . . . Let's do that now. (Pause for a minute.)

And whenever you feel ready, move your fingers and toes and prepare to return to the room . . . and take a deep breath just before opening your eyes.

REASON CAN ANSWER QUESTIONS, BUT IMAGINATION HAS TO ASK THEM.

RALPH GERARD

RELAXATION HAVEN (AGES 6-12)

Begin with the relaxation ritual and focus inwardly.

. . . and as you might wonder . . . really wonder, just what you can discover today . . . you can begin to feel comfortable . . . finding that special place where your body can let go of whatever tensions it needs to let go of . . . so that you can easily find that place where your body can relax and feel good . . . as you breathe in . . . and breathe out . . . and take in a deep breath . . . and slowly exhale . . . and another deep breath . . . and slowly exhale . . . and another . . . good . . . and now find yourself at a pool, where the water is warm . . . just as you like it . . . and it is so inviting to change into a swimsuit and just settle into that warm pool . . . up to your neck . . . the warm water can be relaxing . . . to the legs and feet . . . and to the hips and abdomen . . . and to the chest and arms . . . and do you have any place in your body that needs some attention and love and healing? Because you can have the warmth of the water go right to that place and help it to feel much better . . . to bring healing to it . . . and do you know that you can do that? . . . And you may want to explore how good that warm pool can feel . . . so let's take one minute of clock time, which can be all the inner time you will need to discover just how relaxing it can feel to be in a warm pool of magic water . . . so let's do that now. (Pause for one minute.)

Very good . . . and whenever you feel complete with the exercise, find your way back to the room, taking 30 seconds or so . . . and take a deep breath just before opening your eyes.

TEACHER NOTES AND REMINDERS

1. **Body Stretching and Oxygenating.** With stress-release and calming exercises it is best first to lead students through several minutes of easy stretching movements to help initiate the release-of-stress process in the body. There are suggested exercises in the appendix.

2. **Centering and Calming Exercises.** Select one of the stationary or moving centering exercises from the story line section.

3. **Story Lines.** You may wish to try all of the relaxation story lines to learn which ones your students find most valuable. Within five to seven sessions, many students will be able to move to expanded brain awareness and be functioning in Channels 1 and 2 simultaneously, facilitated by nothing more than the simple sequence of putting three fingers together, taking a deep breath, and focusing inward for fifteen seconds or so.

   After learning this art, students are on their way to more advanced work, learning how to tune to and function from their Learning Channel (3) and their Pattern-Maker/High Creativity Channel (4).

   You and your students may find it interesting to write your own relaxation story lines after several weeks of using those in the book.

4. **Feedback and Class Discussion of the Experiences.** Your sensitive questioning can encourage sharing of experiences. Sharing can be an important and helpful part of the process, because it can help legitimize and validate students' inner experiences. Since sharing of such experiences is not part of the usual format for students, we need to *invite* this "mapping of inner territory" to further enhance wider-spectrum brain accessing.

   For example,

   "How did it feel to take 3 deep breaths?"

   "How did it feel to close your eyes and focus within?"

   "What did it feel like to float on a cloud?"
   (or *whatever the guided experience was*)

HUMAN BEINGS, BY CHANGING THE INNER ATTITUDES OF THEIR MINDS, CAN CHANGE THE OUTER ASPECTS OF THEIR LIVES.

JAMES

MANAGING STRESS AND TENSION FROM THE INSIDE OUT

Have you noticed what happens with your breathing when you tense up over some uncomfortable issue? When we tense up, we tend to breathe in a more shallow manner and, at times, unconsciously hold our breath.

This type of breathing accompanies and *promotes* stress and anxiety. We can frequently release tensions by consciously taking four or five long, deep breaths.

You have likely had personal experience with this. Do you acknowledge it with your students and suggest during tense moments that they take several long, deep breaths to help slow brain waves and facilitate the accessing of channels 3 and 4, which ensures better recall of learned material? A *relaxed* student feels better, learns better, and performs better, and *that* can reduce *teacher* stress and anxiety.

As students become proficient with accessing their fuller brain capabilities, they can become increasingly aware of greater skill in leaving stresses behind, recalling learned material, and developing ease in accessing creative ideas and answers to personal life issues.

NOTHING WE EVER IMAGINED IS BEYOND OUR POWERS, ONLY BEYOND OUR PRESENT SELF-KNOWLEDGE.

THEODORE ROSZAK

THREE-FINGER METHOD FOR RAPIDLY ACHIEVING A CALM MIND-BODY STATE (AGES 8-ADULT)

Explain to students that today you will help them learn another way to speak with their amazing Genius Brain. At times we may need to relax very quickly to enhance our ability to recall something important or regain our inner balance and center. One good strategy for learning rapid relaxation is to program in a "signal button." Demonstrate the three-finger technique by placing the tips of your thumb, index finger, and middle finger of one hand together.

Begin with the relaxation ritual.

This time . . . as you get ready for body and mind calming, find that really comfortable place for yourself now . . . and when you find that good place for your body . . . gently put the fingertips of one of your hands together as you practiced doing . . . now let your hands just be wherever they are comfortable being . . . with three fingers gently together for this exercise . . . and as you find yourself turning your attention inward . . . you can notice how easily your breath comes in and how easily it goes out . . . all by itself . . . as your wise body and mind keep you alive and well . . . and you can trust your mind and body to serve you very well . . . and can be pleasantly surprised with what you can learn to do that can be so useful . . . even while you can relax more and begin to feel really good . . . and can remind your mind and body of a signal that you are creating now . . . a signal to relax very quickly . . . in a matter of seconds . . . because it is important and useful to be able to relax quickly by holding your fingertips together and taking a deep breath . . . and you can surprise yourself as you learn to relax in seconds, using this three-finger signal . . . because your genius brain needs only to be told what you want it

*to do and it learns quickly . . . and you can let this three-finger signal tell
your mind and body to relax immediately and so easily even now . . .*

*We will use this signal many times, and you can learn to relax quickly
. . . and immediately . . . perhaps remembering now . . . something very
funny that happened to you in the past (pause), an event that can come
to your awareness easily now . . . and recalling a funny event from your
past can perhaps let a smile come over your face . . . and in just a moment
I will begin to count from 5 to 1 so that you can return your attention
to the room, feeling amused and relaxed and alert . . . ready for our next
activity. . . .*

The brain hears messages presented while the listener is in a relaxed,
expanded brain function state. Because we avoid directive language and use
only invitational language, students can accept or reject our invitations.

THE ISLAND OF CALM
(AGES 10 AND OLDER)

In this exercise we use our natural ability for imaging to create an inner-
plane "safe place." As quieting thoughts helps to quiet the body via the
release of calming brain hormones, we will use images that suggest quiet
and calmness to permit the body to move in the direction of its preferred
state, that of health and relaxed well-being.

Begin with a comfortable body position and a straight spine, take
several full breaths, and place three fingers together.

*Good, now just let your body breathe you . . . being aware of the air coming
in . . . and the air going out.*

*Now I invite you to take yourself to an island . . . a beautiful and magic
island . . . an Island of Calm . . . a place for you to go with your thoughts
whenever you need to leave stress and tensions behind. (Pause.) Your
island might be a real place you've been to or one you create . . . a beautiful
island . . . There is a protective shield of energy all around your island
that lets **in** love and happy thoughts and keeps **out** all stress and worry
. . . so you are protected here . . . because that shield is powerful and
protects you completely while storms of all sorts can rage around you
. . . As long as you are on your Island of Calm, behind your shield, you
can feel perfectly centered and peaceful. (Pause.)*

*So take yourself there now . . . and get to know your island, because
it is with you all the time . . . and just waiting until it is needed. (Pause.)
When you need to feel safe and centered . . . you can take yourself to your
island instantly . . . and find yourself breathing deeply and slowly and
enjoying the beautiful warm weather there . . . knowing that you are safe,
with a shield around the island that keeps out any stress and any fuss
that might go on around you in your life . . . And can you feel yourself*

to be calm? . . . feeling that stillness . . . now . . . good.

And now, while you are imagining being on your island, with its protective shield . . . perhaps you can imagine something that is usually stressful for you (pause) and can you just begin to allow that image to come to you now? (Pause.) And as you do, take yourself to your island . . . with its protective shield, separate yourself from that stressful image . . . and imagine yourself to be calm and peaceful while that stressful scene rages **outside** *your shield, far away from you? (Pause.) It can be easy for you . . . to view a stressful situation in a different way . . . when you use your powerful mind to take care of you. (Pause.)*

And know that whenever you recognize that you are becoming stressed . . . you can quickly imagine your amazing shield forming immediately around you and your island . . . and protecting you . . . so that you can be calm and still while the stressful situation goes on outside of you . . . and you can feel good with your new ability to remain calm and quiet inside (pause). You can call on this new skill at any time . . . and it can become stronger and stronger each time you call on it . . . to keep you calm and centered inside . . .

Good . . . and now whenever you feel ready, take a deep breath and slowly return your focus to the room . . . and open your eyes.

The last exercise helps develop the art of stepping back from a tense situation (being "witness" to oneself), recentering, and being able to feel secure and calm within. This state is in sharp contrast to what all too frequently occurs when we closely identify with a negative thought or event and as a result, overstress ourselves. If we could step back, remember that we're okay, take a deep breath, and disidentify, we would have a most useful skill. It takes practice, but is it not worth the effort?

You might create variations on this theme, with the same objective in mind. It can be a marvelous service to our students—helping them develop the ability to move through their days handling conflict and being part of the solution rather than part of the problem. Teachers report that many students remember this exercise and, months and years later, thank their teachers for introducing them to a valuable lifetime skill.

ACCESSING THE CREATIVE-INTUITIVE FACULTIES

CREATING A SPECIAL PLACE: THE SANCTUARY (AGES 7-12)

Of the metaphors and images that we can create to allow ourselves to stretch beyond present limits, the inner sanctuary is one of the most useful for both children and adults. With students especially, it has proven an effective key for unlocking "I can't" belief limits. It provides a readily acceptable symbol for a place where we can imagine the new, the supportive, the exciting, the hitherto impossible.

The actual imagery for creating a special place can vary from an initially elaborate story line to (eventually) the simple statement that "it is right over there; let's go explore it." This exercise is an introduction to The Sanctuary and its possibilities. We invite you to encourage your students to create and frequently use this inner expression of their creative faculties, adding new and useful tools and helpers to serve ever-arising life needs.

It can be helpful to introduce the idea of a "safe place" or "sanctuary" or "workshop" or "special place" or whatever terminology suits your students best. If they could create a place where anything was possible in terms of having tools, helpers, models, good advice, inner teachers and coaches, better self-esteem, good feelings, and so on, to what uses might they wish to put their Special Place? They might make personal lists or each work with a friend and explore possibilities.

By this time your students should be able to put three fingers together, take a couple of deep breaths, and take themselves into expanded brain modes. When they are ready, try this introductory story line:

WHAT LIES BEHIND US AND WHAT LIES BEFORE US ARE TINY MATTERS COMPARED TO WHAT LIES WITHIN US.

OLIVER WENDELL HOLMES

Today you can create a very special place for yourself . . . because you may have thought that you would really like to have a place where you could go to have helpers for math lessons and spelling, a coach for sports, a wise person to give you good advice about life issues, friends to remind you of your strong points and just how bright and talented you really are . . . And do you know that you can create such a place in your imagery that can serve you very well with all of that help . . . where all of that can be possible for you? . . . and today's the day to do just that . . . So now you might wish to imagine that beneath your feet is a magic carpet . . . very soft and thick, and as you sit down and get very comfortable, you can think of just where you might like your special place to be . . . And you can even surprise yourself as your magic carpet takes you there . . . like it knew the way by itself . . . so easy . . . to find the most beautiful place you can imagine . . . and I don't know how you will know where that place is, but I do know that as you begin to imagine it . . . you can feel that carpet slowly begin to rise . . . slowly rise . . . slowly, safely, carrying you up and moving you off to your Special Place. (Pause.)

And because your magic carpet is on "automatic pilot" it takes you with amazing speed to your Special Place . . . gently setting you down in this marvelous spot . . . where you can do anything . . . and make anything that you need, to help you be successful . . . and take a good look around now . . . because just over there is a path leading to a workshop . . . a place to make all sorts of things . . . and it's your workshop . . . filled with magic wands and benches and pictures of what you might like to create . . . and see what your workshop looks like . . . Good . . .

Now let's go inside . . . and look around . . . Are you there by yourself or are friends there waiting to greet you? (Pause.) And just over there by the windows is a place where you can design things . . . and there are places for all of your tools so that you can make whatever you can think up (pause) and if you need some help deciding on what you might wish to create . . . there is a big TV screen just over there . . . a big video screen, and ideas of things to make just appear on the screen . . . such as—if you are a skateboard rider, a skateboard can appear on your screen . . . a skateboard that lets you do all the skateboard tricks perfectly . . . or if you are a tennis player—a special racket that lets you make every shot perfectly . . . or if you want to talk to a special person—a pair of earphones that lets you hear the perfect words to say to that special person . . . or perhaps a piano that lets you play the right notes every time and make beautiful music . . .

And would you like to make something in your workshop? . . . Let's make some lights . . . to help you to see well inside the workshop . . . so go outside now . . into the bright sunshine . . . and gather an armful of sun rays . . . picking them carefully to get the ones that are very bright and straight . . . and then cut them so they will be the right size . . . almost as long as your workshop . . . Good . . . Now bring them inside the workshop and carefully place them, one at a time, up on the ceiling . . . and they will stick there easily . . . up on the ceiling . . . Good. (Pause.) And now look around the workshop and see that it is lit up just as brightly as outside . . . with your new sun-ray lights . . . and you can enjoy being in a wonderfully bright light . . . because it can feel good to be in the sunshine . . . warm and calm . . . and now we can leave the workshop for a while . . . and as you go out, you can notice how good you can feel to have a place where you have the tools to make whatever you need to make your life better.

And now what do you want to make to help you be an even better you? (Pause.) And if you thought of something, make it now in your workshop, and then try it out to be sure that it works perfectly. Let's take two minutes of clock time, which can equal all the inner time you will need. What will you make? Let's begin now. (Pause for about 2 minutes.) Good.

Now . . . hop on your magic carpet for a safe and easy ride back here to the classroom . . . and you can count silently to 5 and when you reach 5, take a deep breath . . . and allow your eyes to flutter open, and you can feel refreshed and very good about yourself.

INSPIRATION POINT (AGES 10 YEARS AND OLDER)

This exercise can be used for personal development, stress management, and self-esteem building. It can follow centering and calming exercises. Begin with the usual procedure: comfortable body position, straight spine, soft music, dim lights, good air circulation, quiet classroom environment.

WHEN I EXAMINED MYSELF
AND MY METHODS OF
THOUGHT, I CAME TO THE
CONCLUSION THAT THE GIFT
OF FANTASY HAS MEANT
MORE TO ME THAN MY
TALENT FOR ABSORBING
POSITIVE KNOWLEDGE.

ALBERT EINSTEIN

Each of us at times needs a good friend . . . one who can be there for us and give us good advice . . . so we can find solutions to our problems. You might have an important question in your life right now. Can you think of one? (Pause.) Wouldn't it be good to have a close friend, one who is very wise and who has good advice that will help you to find the best answers to your question? Let's find that wise friend and helper.

Take yourself to your sanctuary . . . your special place of peace and calm . . . your beautiful place . . . a place to feel very good inside . . . and there are many pathways leading from your sanctuary off in different directions . . . all to wonderful places . . . and one path catches your eye now . . . because it is wide and soft, with many flowers . . . and there are fruit trees along the path so that you can eat if you are hungry as you walk along . . . and off in the far distance there is a hill . . . a special hill that you know very well. It is sometimes covered in a lovely glow and the top of the hill is where you can take yourself to discover answers to questions you have about life . . . because the walk along the path to the hill is beautiful . . . with birds singing and nature greeting you as you walk along . . . on a bright sunny day, with gentle breezes swaying the treetops . . . and a few clouds in the sky for you to watch, all the while feeling very good and safe now . . . and as you begin to move up the hill . . . the walk is easy and you might begin to feel full of energy now . . . very alive and good all over . . . like you do when expecting to meet a special friend, someone you like very much . . .

So look up to the top of the hill . . . because it is covered with a lovely glowing light . . . of wonderful colors . . . and you can feel like you do when expecting something very good to happen (pause) while coming to the top of the hill, feeling refreshed and happy . . . there is a small meadow with soft grass . . . and a magnificent view all around . . . and you can see for miles in all directions.

And over there is a tree . . . a large friendly tree that may be familiar to you . . . that is inviting you to come over and rest . . . and sitting on the soft ground with your back against the friendly tree . . . the warmth of the sun can make you feel just a bit sleepy . . . like you want to nod off (pause) and a dreamlike image begins to come to you . . . and in the dream you can notice the figure of something very friendly coming over to you slowly, in a misty cloud . . . and it could be a person or may be an animal or something else . . . because you'll know . . . and it comes to you as a great friend, a wise and caring helper . . . to help you find the answer to your important life question . . . that you can be aware of now . . . and now as the cloud clears the figure becomes clear . . . and you can feel its warmth and its caring for you . . . because it comes to help you to feel safe and loved and to be your friend . . . and as this friend comes closer you can greet one another . . . with happy feelings and great respect . . . and now you have several minutes of clock time equal to all the INNER time you need to meet with your guide and friend and be open to the answers and advice and help that will be offered to you. Remember what you are told so that you can benefit from it in days and weeks to come . . .

So be with your guide now and talk over your question. Let's do that NOW. (Pause for several minutes, then begin speaking very quietly.)

And your conversations can continue . . . perhaps tonight while you're asleep . . . or perhaps you will want to return during your waking times to this place . . . to this friend . . . but for now . . . you may wish to thank your guide for helping . . . perhaps in ways that you are aware of and perhaps in ways that you will become aware of . . . in future days . . . and easily and slowly, beginning to return your awareness now to your body . . . moving fingers and toes . . . and whenever you are ready, take a deep breath . . . and then slowly allow your eyes to open . . . feeling good and ready for our next activities . . .

GANDOLF'S GARDEN (AGES 7-12)

Begin with the usual ritual: comfortable body, straight spine, closed eyes, 3 deep breaths, go inside.

Imagine yourself walking down a forest path . . . on a beautiful mild summer day . . . and there just ahead of you is a mound of freshly dug dirt . . . with a round-topped wooden door on one side . . . which is very, very curious . . . and you might wonder as you approach the door . . . what is on the other side . . . because the door is just slightly ajar . . . so that opening it more fully and looking inside, you can see a tunnel of firm, dry walls. The tunnel is slightly lit . . . apparently from a bright light coming from the other end . . . and the tunnel seems to slope slightly downward . . .

And investigating it further, you find it easy and pleasant walking the tunnel toward the light at the end . . . even as the tunnel brings you deeper and deeper into the Earth . . . and then . . . as the light becomes brighter still . . . the ground turns into a wide children's slide . . . and before you know it . . . there you are sliding down a wonderful slide . . . winding down and dropping into a brightly lit garden . . . coming to rest on a soft spot of grass at the end of the slide . . . at the foot of a grassy knoll . . .

And looking around and up on the knoll you are impressed with the ingenious system of skylights that lighten this marvelous garden . . . and you can hear peals of laughter . . . rather high pitched . . . and turning, you see, standing right there at your elbow, . . . a smiling elf . . . who gestures quite grandly with his staff . . . "I'm Gandolf," he says, "and this is my garden . . . and you are very welcome . . . so feel free to walk around and explore . . . because you are my guest." . . . and then he just disappears . . .

So you stand yourself up . . . dust yourself off . . . and begin to explore this wonderful place . . . and you notice, just off to the right, lovely plants and rocks surrounding a small reflecting pool . . . with shimmering water reflecting the sunlight from far above you . . . while you stand there at the pool, feeling very much at ease and with a slight air of anticipation now . . . becoming aware of the magic of this place . . . as you gaze into the reflecting pool for a few moments . . . and note that there in the pool, gazing back at you is the image of you . . . not as you are . . . but of who you would like to be . . . an ideal you . . . smiling back at you very gently. (Pause for about a minute.)

And you might become aware that this image begins to speak to you . . . in a way that you can understand . . . now . . . speaking to you . . . telling you something about yourself that is important for you to know. (Pause.) Give yourself time to hear this message . . . at some level of your being . . . which might or might not be at your aware level for the moment . . . but the message will be heard. (Pause for about a minute.)

You now move on . . . continuing on the pathway through the colorful and fragrant garden . . . and coming around a bend, you see a little child playing happily, skipping with a rope . . . and that child smiles at you and seems very familiar to you now . . . as you are beckoned to come closer . . . and you can begin to recognize that child to be yourself . . . a part of yourself perhaps forgotten over the years . . . memories of importance to you now in your life . . . some insight you had as a child . . . clear as a bell . . . as children are able to see and hear what is really important . . . and you bend down so you can hear or see or feel . . . that message that is important for you now . . . so listen. (Pause.)

And the child then skips happily away, leaving you perhaps with feelings of love. (Pause.) And you follow along the path, through a clearing with bright butterflies and songbirds flying around your head joyously . . . singing their own message on their wings . . . and reaching now almost the end of the path . . . where you notice an old person sitting cross-legged just before the path ends . . . who appears to be meditating . . . but as you approach, the person's eyes slowly open, twinkling . . . as if expecting you . . . and once again . . . that familiar look . . . that draws you so strongly . . . perhaps the recognition that this, too, is you . . . in your days of wisdom and inner peace . . . speaking to you from your own future . . . as an issue of importance in your life might come effortlessly to mind now . . . an issue of importance . . . that can be viewed and perhaps solved with a view from the future (pause) so that issue might be resolved now . . . as the old person beckons you to come nearer and communicates to you in a manner you can understand . . . the solution to that life issue . . . that insight that is so helpful can come to you now. (Pause for about a minute.)

Knowing that the response . . . that insight . . . can come to you at any time . . . and may surprise you over the next few days . . . unless of course it has already come to you . . . you can move on further, completing your tour of the gardens and returning to the grassy area where Gandolf awaits you . . . with a smile and telling you that it is time for you to return to the outside world once again.

The questions and messages of the garden experience can be revealed to you at the most appropriate time and place by your deeper mind . . . so that you can be pleasantly surprised with the insights awaiting you . . . and you might thank Gandolf . . . as you turn to go back up an easy path . . . taking with you certain awarenesses . . . and slowly . . . as you find yourself completed with this journey . . . and whenever you are ready . . . allowing your eyes to flutter open . . . returning your awareness to this room . . . perhaps recalling some of the insights and answers now imprinted in your deeper mind.

I FOUND THAT I COULD SAY THINGS WITH COLOR AND SHAPES THAT I HAD NO WORDS FOR.

GEORGIA O'KEEFFE

9

FULL ESTEEM AHEAD: BUILDING SELF-ESTEEM*

Learning is enhanced by a calm mind, a relaxed body, and an attitude that says *"I can do that!"* Our beliefs and attitudes about ourselves (our self-image or self-esteem) set us up for success or something less than success. One of the more important uses of imagery is in creating positive self-esteem via "mind videos" that say *"I am capable!"*

One successful approach for enhancing self-esteem is to encourage learners to create special inner-plane helpers who have the power to help us be successful as both learners and performers on the stage of life. These helper images, when imaged in a relaxed state, become messages to the Pattern Maker of the brain to get busy creating a new pattern designed to lead us to positive experiences represented by the helper metaphor. An inner helper can thus allow us to give ourselves permission to accept that we *can* do something and do it well. It creates an inner attitude or brain pattern, which in turn influences future outer behavior and experience. We all create helpers or helper attitudes in our lives. For example, we "psych" ourselves up before an athletic event or theater performance, preen before the vanity mirror before going out, or mentally rehearse how we will ask for a raise. What is a helper if not a model or an intermediate that sets us up for possible success by giving us confidence?

Most children love having personal confidantes, special friends known only to them-selves—allies who will take up their cause, to whom they can pour out their troubles, who offer helpful suggestions, and who serve as models. Young children often use favorite toys, pets, or imaginary friends as allies. The imaginary friend can take almost any form at any age. As long as the help and support is a product of our *inner process,* our *inner reality,* it is conducive to building self-esteem and is a worthy exercise in accessing intuitive, creative inner resources.

*WITH THANKS TO MARTHA HEIBERG, WHOSE CREATIVE BRAIN CAME UP WITH THIS TITLE.

Because our adult process is frequently just the opposite of children's, we as educators may not acknowledge the value of the child's process. As adults, we frequently create powerful real-life rather than imaginary helpers (the doctor, mechanic, sports hero, and so on) without having a cadre of inner helpers to bolster our confidence to create our desired results. That process of *externalizing* power can leave us feeling helpless rather than empowered, and thus less able to cope successfully with our daily issues.

CHOOSING OUR ILLUSIONS

For years now, the psychological literature has led us to believe that the well-adjusted person is one who assesses reality accurately and operates from these assessments. Conversely, the person who operates primarily from personal illusions about self is more likely to be poorly adjusted, with a greater tendency to instability and social failure.

However, *researchers have found that our illusions affect our experiences, and that certain illusions are actually conducive to positive mental health and social success and well-being.*

Researchers find that positive illusions may be useful, and they cite data showing that cancer patients with a sense of personal control over their illness demonstrate a superior psychological adjustment to their disease, regardless of outcome. Further, a positive self-image allows people to manage negative feedback constructively and without great upset. Taylor and Brown (1988) report that "the mentally healthy person appears to have the enviable capacity to distort reality [hold illusions] in a direction that *enhances* self-esteem, maintains beliefs in personal efficacy and promotes an *optimistic* view of the future."

Such positive self-images seem to *promote* mental health, the capacity for personal happiness and contentment, and the ability to be productive and creative in daily work. As Taylor and Brown state, "Certain biases in perception that have previously been thought of as amusing peccadillos at best and serious flaws in information-processing at worst may actually be highly adaptive under many circumstances. *Positive* illusions help make each individual's world a warmer and more active and beneficial place in which to live" (emphasis added).

We suggest that it is just this innate ability to influence our outer experiences through our inner thoughts, attitudes, and "illusions" that is our human neurologic heritage and that allows us to expand beyond our apparent limits at any age. Since we help to create our personal *limits* with our illusions, we can also foster the development of illusions that take us beyond our learned limits, with images that help create the positive outcomes we desire.

With Positive Outcome Patterning, we help our students access the "illusion builder" (Pattern Maker) directly and suggest, via our story lines, the building of positive, useful attitudes about our identity, our

TO LOOK AT THE WORLD FROM A NEW PERSPECTIVE IS TO DISCOVER A WORLD OF NEW POSSIBILITIES.

STANISLAV GROF

capabilities, and our vision for future success and happiness. These thought-forms can be "anchored in" as positive expectations and new belief systems, which tend to become self-fulfilling prophecies in our lives.

INDIRECT SUGGESTION FOR CHANGE OF BEHAVIOR

HOW IT WORKS IN THE CLASSROOM

It is frequently more useful and successful to request behavior changes indirectly. We can make such requests by being advisors to the rational, logical brain while it is in communication with the intuitive, creative part, or in other words, while students are in expanded brain states.

One effective tool for indirect requests or invitation is *highlighting*. In other words, we make a specific request stand out from the rest of the sentence in any of several verbal or nonverbal ways.

1. Pause before or after the highlighted words or phrases.
2. Take a longer time to utter the invitational words.
3. Raise or lower your voice's pitch or volume for the invitational words.
4. As indicated on the audiocassette, you are invited to identify a highlighting procedure that is best for you. Once you have identified it, use it consistently with your students.

SEEDING SUGGESTIONS

What can we do in the classroom environment to help students academically by gaining more direct and effective access to their *Learning Channel?* An enjoyable way to reach both the Learning and Pattern-Maker Channels is to use a story into which you, the facilitator, weave seed suggestions. The suggestions invite students to use their vast neurologic resources to discover a new, better way of doing something and to try it out in a safe and comfortable environment. Our brains can and do perform this service for us: reviewing our past experiences, selecting useful pieces, and reassembling them in new and novel ways that provide insights and answers to our life issues and better ways of being in the world.

In creating stories, we recommend that you suggest what to do in a general way (provide context without much content). We do not know what each student selects as a personal issue to work with, and with our suggestion-seeding approach we need not know details about another person's life in order to offer suggestions that can be useful. We thus respect the privacy and integrity of our students' personal lives.

This approach engages the interest of the Action Channel while invoking communication with the higher-resource Learning and Pattern-

IN ONESELF LIES THE WHOLE WORLD AND IF YOU KNOW HOW TO LOOK AND LEARN, THEN THE DOOR IS THERE AND THE KEY IS IN YOUR HAND. NOBODY ON EARTH CAN GIVE YOU EITHER THE KEY OR THE DOOR TO OPEN, EXCEPT YOURSELF.

J. KRISHNAMURTI

Maker Channels. These channels are also the home of our innate problem-solving abilities. When we encourage students to function from their more expanded brain faculties, we provide them with opportunities to access a smooth flow of creative, intuitive input while simultaneously being in tune with their reason, logic, analytic, Channel 1 mode. *It is this ability to function at will in multiple brain modes that is a critical mark of the fully functioning human.*

Let's weave such a story now.

USING DIRECT IMAGERY FOR OTHER POSITIVE OUTCOMES

PREPARATION FOR TALKING TO A GROUP

Preparing for a talk before a live audience provides a good opportunity to use imagery for rehearsal. Response to this exercise has been very enthusiastic. (We are most interested in how students perceive themselves and their sense of the entire experience.) Students report easier recall of information, an increased sense of calm, feelings of support from the audience, and good feelings about the delivery of the talks.

Begin with the usual relaxation ritual.

*To create a talk, you'll need a lot of information . . . Easy . . . let an image just drift up into your **awareness of** all the **information you need,** . . . being "out there" somewhere . . . maybe on videotapes, or maybe in books in a library, or maybe in other people's heads . . . all the information you need to prepare a really great talk (pause) and now . . . begin to imagine how all of this **information will come to you** . . . and do the words fly off pages, and maybe whole sentences march off the pages like soldiers into your head, or from videotapes, or out of people's heads . . . and pour into your head? . . . Do you have a little door in your head for all this information to come in . . . just effortlessly . . . and so easy in your imagery . . . or perhaps as you touch the book or tape to your head, the proper information enters your brain (pause) or maybe your **own image** will come to you . . . of how easy it is for the **information** you need to **gather** . . . to **come to you** now . . . Do you **see it?** or do you **talk to yourself** about it happening? or do you feel it? It's all the same . . . And then can you **imagine** . . . your brain **sorting it** all out and **storing it** so it can **feed it back** to you **as you need it** . . . and all neatly stored in your memory library inside your head. (Pause.)*

*So there you are now **creating your talk** . . . and the **information** you need is **coming to you now,** filling your head . . . and how **easy** it seems to be . . . and how **good** you can **feel** just sitting there and **learning** all the while. (Pause.) And I don't know how you will **get** that **information you need** to **prepare your talk** and **do it very well***

*. . . and you may be **pleasantly surprised** . . . **surprise yourself** to **discover** how **talented** you are in **getting it all together** into a very good talk . . . and you can **feel** very **good** about that . . .*

*Now imagine your **head filled** with the information you need . . . while you sit at your table or desk or wherever . . . and now you need to put it on paper . . . and to actually write it (or type it) out . . . so **let an image come** to you effortlessly, of you writing (or typing) all that good information . . . while just the right **words flow** onto the paper . . . and it seems to do so almost by itself . . . with just the **right words** . . . and in just the **right order** . . . to **make** a really **good presentation** . . . and in your imagination page after **page fills** and a **wonderful talk** is taking shape . . . right before your eyes . . . and how easy to **do good work** just **letting** your **talented, creative** brain **do** the **work** . . . and putting all the good ideas on paper . . . because calling on your creative brain is easy . . . just **let it know** what you want it to do . . . like we are doing now . . . **with images** . . . because that's how to **communicate with** brain . . . Good.*

Now . . . let that image fade . . . count yourself slowly from 1 to 5, take a deep breath, and . . . feeling very good now . . . like a large task is already completed . . . and allow yourself to slowly return your awareness to the classroom.

IMAGES TO ENHANCE STUDY (AGES 10 AND OLDER)

ROOM PREPARATION

1. Quiet music, preferably a classical selection
2. Good air circulation
3. Comfortable sitting position. Begin with the typical relaxation ritual and a centering exercise.

*Later today you will go home, and **nice things can happen** . . . and sometime today you will want to **review the studies** we have done here in class today . . . Now I'm not sure how you will **find** that **right time and quiet place** that will help you to **learn easily,** but I do know that you might want to **remember what we did** here today . . . and while you are **feeling good and relaxed,** you might **let** a mind **picture form** now . . . of you **finding** that **right place** where you can **recall what** we **learned** today. (Pause.)*

*Imagine how easy it can be to **go** right **to the learning place** inside your head . . . where you can **remember what is important to know** . . . and I know you can **do this very well** . . . and imagine **learning quickly and thoroughly** . . . because it can **feel good** to know that you are a **fast learner** and have a wonderful, intelligent mind that* *learns quickly* and very well . . . and you may be pleasantly surprised to *discover new abilities* and new learnings as your mind *knows how to learn* what you need to know here . . . and *do it easily* and *quickly* . . . so you can *feel good* that you have *reviewed what we did today* and *remember it* very well . . .

So now think of someone you really like . . . and perhaps a smile can begin as you think of that person and you can feel good all over.

PREPARING FOR AN EXAM

It is best for students to do this exercise being guided by the facilitator or listening to it on a tape. It assumes the ability to voluntarily slow waves to an alpha level or slower.

Put your thumb and two fingers of one hand together now, and take yourself to your alpha levels . . . Bring in the image of your sanctuary now . . . Good. Seat yourself in your sanctuary . . . in preparation for some important work . . . This work can help you to move through your life more smoothly . . . more successfully, easily, confidently, comfortably . . . Our focus is on success . . . the successful you . . .

Now . . . let a screen appear to you . . . on which you can call up an image of a person . . . The screen appears out in front of you, and there . . . now . . . on that screen, you can see yourself . . . sitting in a classroom . . . sitting at a desk, and your eyes are partially closed . . . and you are perfectly relaxed . . . and you can watch yourself up there on the screen, and your body can feel very comfortable and quiet . . . you perhaps have a slight smile on your face . . . because you are so easy and calm.

And you recognize that you are there to have a successful experience with some questions . . . that the teacher will ask you . . . on paper . . . and you are ready for these questions . . . because you have prepared well for them . . . and can find that the answers to the questions will come easily and quickly to you . . . and you can know the correct answers easily . . . and can put those correct answers on your exam paper . . . because the answers to those questions are stored neatly inside your brain's memory banks . . . and you know how you call them up when you need them . . . and you can be relaxed and calm now . . . while the exam paper comes to you . . . with the slight smile on your face . . . You can begin the exam.

So do a quick scan of the questions . . . to discover that they are easy and that you already know the answers very well (pause) just sitting there now, you can answer those questions . . . because they are so easy, and you know . . . that you will do very well . . . while you watch yourself now, answering each question . . . one at a time (pause). Good . . . Now complete the entire exam . . . and when finished . . . you can sit back feeling calm and good, knowing that you have done very well . . . Good . . .

Now . . . let that scene fade . . . and put yourself at the same desk about a week later as the teacher hands out the grades . . . the marks . . . and how your face smiles as you see that you received very high marks . . . and are feeling good about you . . . and about your ability to learn very well . . . and learn very well how to take an exam successfully . . . easily . . . and score high marks . . . Good . . . Now take a deep breath and count yourself from 1 to 5 . . . slowly returning your awareness to this room.

FULL ESTEEM AHEAD: MORE EXERCISES FOR PROMOTING SELF-ESTEEM

"SMART COOKIE" YOU (AGES 9 AND OLDER)

We all have a voice inside us that is self-critical. When we goof, it calls us names and we feel less than okay. Because that voice is a loud one for most of us, it is very important that we also have a voice inside that congratulates us when we do well. "Smart cookie you are," it might say, or "Well done!" or "You can feel good about that!"

In this exercise we will treat ourselves to time on the Smart Cookie Train, which takes us to Smart Cookie Land, where we get to acknowledge what we do really well, how we help others, and how we can reward ourselves with some nice treats that we deserve to have.

So . . . get comfortable . . . spine straight . . . 3 fingers together . . . 3 deep breaths . . . go inside.

Get yourself down to the train station . . . there it is . . . with the long platform that the trains pull up to . . . and your train is there . . . the happiest looking train you've seen . . . all painted up in bright colors, like a circus . . .

Smiling, happy people are getting on board . . . people who are able to say that they may not be perfect, but that they do some things really well. In fact, your ticket for this train is to identify something about yourself that even you have to admit . . . is special and excellent . . . so **find** *that* **quiet place within** *you . . . now . . .* **clear** *your* **thoughts** *and simply* **allow** *a* **thought or feeling to come** *to you that tells you something nice about you . . . something that you can* **feel** *very* **good** *about . . . Allow that to come to your awareness. (Pause for 30 seconds.)*

Good . . . that's your ticket for the train. It gets you aboard the Smart Cookie Train . . . so hop aboard now . . . and in just a few moments, you'll be off to Smart Cookie Land . . . and good times . . .

So as you step up into that happy train, look around you and notice how people look and how they act when they feel okay, **feel calm and centered within** *themselves, and show that in their faces (pause) and* *you* can *do that* too (pause) because as you enter the train, you **become** one of the **calm and centered** people, **with love** for yourself and for others . . . and you can **feel welcomed** aboard, as someone helps you find a comfortable seat . . . and you can **feel** very **wanted and special** . . . Once you are comfortable you can begin to welcome others aboard and help them **feel wanted** . . .

And the train begins to move . . . and pick up speed . . . and you can feel an air of **expectation** as you begin to imagine what it is like in Smart Cookie Land, where you get to **enjoy doing** things well, for yourself and for others. (Pause for 30 seconds.)

In fact, in just a few minutes you'll be coming into the station, so you might look out the train window to get a view of what the land looks like. People who live here **do** just **what** they **want to do** . . . **what** they really **enjoy doing,** for themselves and for others . . . and that's one reason they **do** everything so **well** . . . because they **love what** they are doing . . . and you can **think of what you love to do** . . . and **do well,** and can begin to **feel good** all over . . . (Pause for 30 seconds.)

Coming into the station you can see a crowd of people there to greet you all . . . someone to greet everyone on the train . . . Stepping out onto the station platform, you can spot a warm smile as someone approaches you . . . greets you by your name . . . and welcomes you to The Land . . . Perhaps you can hear that person say that he or she has been expecting you to come . . . so you can **discover** what a **good** and **clever person you** really **are** . . . and allow yourself to **feel** very **good** inside . . . knowing that you do have special talents and that **you are lovable** and a **good person** . . . just the way you are now . . .

So in a moment, you'll have some time to imagine yourself **doing what** you **like to do,** and **doing it** very **well** . . . and let's take 2 minutes of clock time, which will be just what you need of inner time to imagine yourself **doing what** you really **like to do,** and **doing it** very **well** . . . let's begin that . . . now. (Pause for 2 minutes, then begin speaking quietly.)

So . . . you might just note how **good** you can **feel** in this land . . . and even know that The Land is part of you . . . and that it would be good to take yourself on a ride on that Smart Cookie Train frequently . . . just to remind yourself that you can **do what you** really **like to do,** and that **you are** a **special person** . . . special to yourself . . . and special to others . . .

As you guide your students back to focusing in the classroom you might allow your own brain to present you with useful ways to connect this self-esteem exercise with other activities so that students can activate their imagery in a life-relevant way.

VARIATIONS OF THE THEME

1. Identify something that you can do but would like to do better. Imagine doing it perfectly.

2. Identify something you think you cannot do now but would like to be able to do—and do well. Imagine yourself doing that, happily and elegantly.
3. Think of someone that you'd like to do something nice for . . . some special favor . . . some special gift. Imagine doing it.
4. Think of something you would like to do or have for yourself that would not be at anyone else's expense. Imagine doing or having it and enjoying it fully.

IDEAL-YOU EXERCISE (AGES 8 AND OLDER)

Here is another exercise to enhance self-esteem and to help students recognize and own their power to shape their inner and outer experiences. Effects improve with repetition. It has proven an excellent exercise for dealing with the "poor-little-me" attitude in which we all seem to get stuck periodically. Begin with the relaxation ritual and direct students to their workshops.

Now that you are in your workshop, sit in your most comfortable place where you can see the life-size screen in front of you . . . Now, everyone has a model of who they really want to be like . . . Do you know who you'd like to be . . . or maybe have an ideal person who is a good model for you? If you could suddenly turn into your ideal self . . . what would you look like and how would you act in the world? Well, you can find out right now . . .

You'll need to follow these directions carefully . . . Imagine yourself up there on your screen . . . dressed the way you usually dress . . . and try to act like you want to act, but not succeeding . . . and watch yourself on the screen not succeeding.

Okay . . . now talk to that person on the screen like a good friend . . . very sympathetically . . . and tell that person up there on the screen that you will help in just a minute . . . now let that image fade . . .

In your workshop you have a magic wand . . . that permits you to change any scene . . . now take your wand . . . it sparkles . . . and slowly let a new image of yourself come up on that screen . . . an image of you that you really want to be . . . looking just great . . . dressed in the way you know you look good . . . and now you can walk just right . . . and you can speak in that perfect voice . . . When you walk by, people turn around and look at you with admiration and respect because you have a beautiful smile, and you share it wherever you go . . . and note how people respond to that smile . . . They smile back at you . . . and it feels great . . . and note how you stand and walk. It is amazing how good your posture is when you're feeling good about yourself . . . And how are people responding to you? Can you see the smiles on their faces when they look your way . . . admiringly . . . because they appreciate you for who you are . . . a fine person . . . Good . . .

Okay . . . now, if that all feels okay, in a moment you can jump into that body . . . get right inside it . . . and be that person . . . Good. Now jump inside your own body on the screen, and let it turn into a live scene and you are in your new, confident body . . . and looking good and feeling good . . . because down inside you are good with lots of charm and confidence, so easy with no effort at all. (Pause.)

And where would you like to go for a while where you can have some good times? . . . And you can feel very close to people . . . and know that they like you a lot . . . and you like them . . . because you can go there now . . . feeling close to other people . . . and feeling good inside yourself . . . and you can go there now. (Pause.)

And now imagine your body beginning to glow with light . . . the light getting brighter . . . and spreading out from you like sunshine . . . shining on everyone around you now . . . And they can feel relaxed and easy just like you do . . . all of you glowing with a sunshine light and feeling amazingly good . . . because it's so nice to feel that closeness with your friends . . .

Good . . . Now keep that good feeling . . . and slowly count yourself from 1 to 5 and come on back to the room . . . feeling very good . . .

GENERATING ORIGINAL IDEAS

This exercise is one of a series designed to stimulate our natural capacity to create beyond what we consider our "normal" limits. As with other exercises in this book, it is best to put it into your own words and phrases. Use our words here only as guidelines.

We suggest that students work in groups of three for the sharing part of this exercise, to stimulate one another's thinking process and to establish a trust circle. You may also wish to have students work as a full class if the trust level is very high.

Help students in your group into their relaxed, centered mode and then offer these suggestions:

Good . . . now that you can find yourself in that very relaxed place . . . that place where you can feel very good inside yourself . . . and ready to explore some of your Genius Brain talents . . . you may wish to take yourself to your Sanctuary . . . your Special Place . . . where you can call on your amazing abilities so easily, . . . and you may wish to call on helpers for this exercise . . . to help you let ideas come to you easily . . . because in a few moments I will ask you to imagine one or two maybe wild ideas . . . ideas for things or events that probably don't exist on the planet right now . . . and as those ideas might come to you . . . allow them to grow . . . so that you can get an entire video of what's happening . . . and how

EVERYBODY HAS WON, AND
ALL MUST HAVE PRIZES.

LEWIS CARROLL

it all works . . . and then you can be so pleased and perhaps surprised as those ideas can come to you easily.

So now if you can find yourself in the best place now at your Sanctuary . . . the best place for getting new ideas . . . where might you be? (Pause for 30 seconds.) And getting comfortable now and clearing your mind of all thoughts . . . just allowing thoughts to clear . . . so that your head can feel light and bright (30-second pause) and ready to easily receive ideas from your Genius Brain.

And now it can be fun to allow yourself to begin to imagine a wild idea (30-second pause) and perhaps allow that idea to grow into a scene for you . . . that can be very satisfying and enjoyable . . . and taking one minute of clock time, which can be equal to all the inner time you need, to allow impossible ideas to develop in your thoughts . . . and really enjoy it. (Pause for one minute, then quietly resume.)

Good . . . and in a few moments we will gently return our focus to the room, where we can share whatever idea or ideas came to you . . . so now . . . (Guide students back to room focus, reminding them to take a deep breath just before opening eyes.)

Once your students get the idea of simply allowing new and fresh ideas to come to them, the applications are certainly limitless. Variations on the theme could be getting ideas for science projects, school or class fund-raiser activities, new play group equipment design, a better way to learn math, a playground game, how to better use classroom and school space, and so on. You can have fun allowing your own Genius Brain to come up with additional variations.

With this type of exercise, we invite our students to enter the exciting world of invention and original thinking. Such work requires a degree of stillness of thoughts, a playfulness of mind, and total open-endedness, with as little teacher definition and involvement as possible. If you are consistent in accepting all student responses with the same enthusiasm and nonjudgmental attitude, exercises such as this can help you to bring new magic to your classroom. From here it is but a short step to imagining being successful academically. Before a lesson, for example, students might be asked to imagine success with the lesson material.

YOUR NATURAL "TUNING-IN" TIME

During every 24-hour period there is at least one special time when your rational brain and your super-brain are in close communication. If you can identify this time and use it with purpose and awareness, you can reach into your own great potential and get it working for you in marvelous ways that can pleasantly surprise you.

When might that time be? Well, you'll need to discover it for yourself, as it differs among people. To discover it, search for a time, day or night, when you are calm and quiet and your busy self-talk is quite still. If this time occurs during daytime hours you will likely be involved in a simple activity that allows your thoughts to wander quietly. You might be in the shower, in the garden, washing dishes, walking the dog, or possibly in meditation or prayer. The time might also be just as you are falling asleep or as you are waking.

You will know this is your Tuning-in Time if ideas come to you effortlessly, solutions to problems seem to appear out of nowhere, new insights and good ideas pop into your awareness. When does this time occur for you? Maybe you can identify that time now.

This time can be a uniquely valuable period of your day. During this time your usual awareness and your deep awareness (Channels 1, 3, and 4) are naturally in synch, communicating clearly with each other. If you learn how and when to use this Tuning-in Time, it can change your life for the better.

You can use this time

1. To present issues and problems to your super-brain, to encourage it to get to work to bring you an answer. You do this naturally, but less efficiently, when you think about a problem you are having, then after a while give up trying with your Channel 1 brain to figure it out, and then "sleep on it." When you are asleep, your super brain can get to work on the issue without interference from Channel 1, which thinks it is so smart but really is not very smart at all, in contrast to your super brain (Channel 3 and Channel 4).
2. To allow your attention to focus inwardly so that you can be available to your super brain to receive its ideas, solutions, and insights.

Identify this tuning in time for yourself and start to use it. Make it a habit; you'll be very pleased that you did.

WILL THIS CLOSE-COMMUNICATION TIME OCCUR ONLY DURING WAKING HOURS?

Not necessarily. At times, your super-brain might awaken you in the middle of the night, and you will find yourself to be quite alert. At such a time, with stillness all around you, you can more readily remain focused within yourself and be in excellent communication with your Channel 3 and Channel 4 abilities.

With a bit of self-suggestion, you can remain awake for 30 minutes or more, do some excellent creative/productive work, and return to sleep, awakening refreshed the next morning, without missing that sleep time at all. In fact, you may wish to explore sleeping for about four hours at one stretch, taking a 15- to 30-minute magic, creative, middle-of-the-night break, and returning to sleep for another several hours or so. If you decide to do this, suggest to your super brain (as you are falling asleep), that it awaken you at night at your best time for creative work. As you return to sleep after this period, suggest to your brain that it awaken you in the morning refreshed and ready for a great day.

Sleeping and waking in this manner is more in agreement with our natural cycles. We do not optimally function "full-on" for eight hours straight, as we might be expected to do in the workplace or during sleep time. Allowing for more natural waking and sleeping cycles puts us in better communication with our super brain.

10

USING OUR BRAINS FOR A CHANGE

"CARPE DIEM!"

"Seize the day!" Not a bad rally cry—quite good, really. It might be called a message of our age, urging us to take back responsibility for our daily thoughts, words, and actions, which, according to quantum theory, appear to affect the entire physical universe. In the language of poetry we are told that we cannot but pick a flower without changing the balance of the universe. Or, as I reflected in "Notes to the Universe,"

> *We "do" the world through magic glass,*
> *Though see not thoughts and feelings pass;*
> *Or watch them pierce our rainbow screens,*
> *As Universe rise in dreams.*
> *Might we, while one with Vital Force,*
> *Awake to catch a glimpse of Source?*
> *To know with what we play and prod,*
> *As we watch God, discover God.*

We do have exercises, easy to learn and easy to practice, that can demonstrate to us the power of our thoughts to affect our experiences in daily living. Considering the large number of life interests and areas in which this is already being demonstrated (in health and sports, for example), it is surprising that educators have not more definitively investigated ways to get on such a worldwide scientific bandwagon. To subtly prod such investigation, we take directed imagery to the next stage, offering additional, practical classroom-based exercises wherein both students and educators can observe for themselves how we can use our brains for a positive change.

POSITIVE OUTCOME PATTERNING: PUTTING IT TO WORK

Positive Outcome Patterning involves self-change, initiated by students for their own benefit, under your guidance and suggestion. We can work with the Pattern Maker part of our brains in any area of life in which we wish to contribute actively for better future outcomes. Areas in which P.O.P. is useful include the following:

- **Managing Personal Stress:** We become able to shed tensions, relax the body, and quiet the "chattering monkey" thought process.

- **Feeling Better about Ourselves:** For raising self-esteem using P.O.P. tools, we focus on our strengths and assets and our power to change ourselves rather than focusing on our inadequacies and powerlessness or attempts to change others. Cultural, social, and religious values all too frequently encourage us to focus on our weaknesses and inadequacies. We then oblige the culture and proceed to strengthen those inadequacy programs by using our imaginations to create repeated images of what's wrong with us and how ineffective we are to change ourselves.

Schooling frequently supports a focus on what *isn't* working rather than on what *is* working, where its clients need to improve rather than where they excel. Interestingly, we know of no body of research (other than the New Zealand–developed Reading Recovery Program) showing that remedial work produces better results than allowing students to focus on their strengths, build their self-esteem, and learn what they need to know at their own speed.

- **Interpersonal Relations:** We can only be as accepting and as loving of others as we are accepting and loving of ourselves. Most of us would like to be more successful with friendships and to feel more fulfilled via those friendships. The classroom can be a setting to facilitate helping students to learn the importance of positively directing their thought self-talk in a way that supports and builds their self-esteem and self-acceptance.

- **Personal Inquiry:** As children, we arrived for our first experience of schooling with our natural zest for discovery and firsthand exploration operating quite successfully. Within a few years of school training, as we were gradually required to absorb more and more secondhand information in the classroom, with the joy of self-discovery and initiation of our own learning experiences gradually removed from the schooling format, many of us also gradually lost the art and practice of self-motivated learning. We became accustomed to teacher-initiated learning. When in later years, we were

MUCH ENERGY IS USUALLY DIRECTED TOWARD MANIPULATION AND CONTROL OF THE EXTERNAL ENVIRONMENT, AND OF OTHER PEOPLE. IF WE TURN THAT ENERGY INWARD TOWARD SELF-OBSERVATION WE CAN DISCOVER HOW TO TRANSFORM OUR EXPERIENCE ... BY CHANGING NOT OUR EXTERNAL PROPS BUT OUR STATE OF CONSCIOUSNESS.

PARAPHRASED FROM FRANCIS E. VAUGHN

expected to take responsibility for our own learning, many of us demonstrated difficulty, having lost this art due to the schooling process itself.

You can be effective in helping students return to the joy of self-discovery and to taking responsibility for their own learning with both P.O.P work and with the Challenge Learning approaches presented here. You are invited to use these approaches in your classroom learning environment and note the results for yourself.

🕸 **Performance in Sports:** The methods recommended here are used in sport training for Olympic athletes and by coaches and athletes worldwide.

🕸 **Academic Achievement:** We perform better in any challenge when relaxed and confident. Conducting a three-minute P.O.P. session before lessons, quizzes, student presentations, in-class projects, and so on, can significantly improve academic performance.

🕸 **Accessing Creativity and Original Thinking:** We all have vast, untapped creative reserves (Goldberg 1983; Healy 1990; Lozanov 1978; Ornstein 1987). To access these reserves requires mastery of specific skills, including stilling thoughts, holding a clear image or vision of what we wish to achieve, and learning the *personal* language *symbols* of communication that our brain uses to bring creative insights to our awareness. The P.O.P. methods in this book are designed to help educators reawaken students to these skills so they might better learn to access creative processes *on call* rather than in the usual unpredictable manner.

TOOLS FOR CHANGE (AGES 8 TO ADULT)

In this and the following exercises, students can demonstrate their own power for positive change. As you know, the approaches and exercises offered in this book are intended to empower the user, enhance self-esteem, promote positive accomplishments, and create pleasurable life experiences. In this series, you will be introducing students to *reframing*, an effective and change-inducing tool. As the song says,

> *You've got to accentuate the positive,*
> *eliminate the negative . . .*
> *and don't mess with Mr. In-between.*

The media provide us with large and powerful doses of negativity, violence, and general demeaning of life. The exercises in this book can provide you and your students with a refreshing diet of positive mind activities. The exercises are something like the ideal pain reliever: they go to work quickly, bring comfort effectively, cost nothing, and are readily available.

If imagery can bring about a nervous stomach or a calm body, poor memory or excellent recall, athletic mediocrity or expanded physical performance, what might it do with the everyday "stone walls" in our lives? What are the stone walls in your students' lives? Given an opportunity to list the "top 10 complaints in my life," students can readily uncover these resistance areas. We now have classroom-based tools to work with them, so let's do just that.

ONE APPROACH: IMAGE FLIP OR REFRAMING (AGES 10 TO ADULT)

1. Have students, as a group, list what is not working for them in their lives. Put each complaint into the form of a sentence and write that sentence on the board (draw a vertical line down center of the board and write complaints on left side). This part of the exercise is "identifying the stone walls."

2. Have the class restate each complaint in the most *positive* form they can, and write it, in one sentence, to the right of the vertical line, across from the negative complaint. For example, across from the complaint "I feel ugly" would be the opposite, "I feel beautiful."

3. Demonstration: Get a student volunteer (or you can demonstrate). In one minute, the student tells the class her complaint. Then classmates suggest what the positive-opposite version of her complaint might be. The student listens to the suggestions and then states her positive version in one sentence.

    The student then "goes inside" (eyes open or closed) and allows images to flow into her mind. She states her ideal scenario, *in first person:* what she is doing as if she were living the positive version then and there. The more elaborate and dramatic, the better. This process should take up to three minutes. The volunteer's task is to allow herself to take the issue to its *wildest* positive fantasy, verbally sharing it with the rest of the class, allowing herself to feel happiness, success, pleasure, love, joy, and so on. For example, she might win a first prize as a dancer in a contest, or win an Olympic gold medal as an athlete. As a student, she might earn an "A" on the next exam.

4. Once the idea is clear to all, divide the class into groups of three. One person in each group serves as speaker. The other two help reframe the speaker's complaint into a one-sentence positive or flip version. One also serves as timekeeper, who gives the speaker three minutes, and one as monitor, who keeps the speaker in first-person, present-tense mode.

    It will take a bit of practice for students to allow themselves to free their image flow while "on stage." Every class should have one or two hams who, if kept on focus, can serve as good modelers for the exercise. As with all exercises, this one will work beautifully for some, who may report dramatic personal changes, when they stay with it, repeating it daily for two weeks. Others may not find it their cup of tea, and that's just fine; they may find some other exercises to suit their needs better.

EXERCISES FOR CHANGING NEGATIVE SELF-TALK AND FEELINGS

REFRAMING (AGES 10 TO ADULT)

Sample instructions to students follow:

We have many thoughts and feelings that we dwell on from time to time about how unhappy we are with ourselves. Perhaps we think about how we appear less than beautiful to others. Perhaps we think we weigh too much or too little. Maybe we would like to be able to meet someone but know we'd feel too shy to walk up and say hello.

The next exercises contain tools you can use to be more successful in your own life and achieve more of your goals. You are a powerful creator already, though you probably aren't aware of that fact. By using the talents you already have, you can discover for yourself how good you can be in making your goals come true.

IT WAS A MENTAL STATE OF HAPPINESS ABOUT AS COMPLETE AS I HAVE EVER KNOWN. IDEAS CAME IN AN UNINTERRUPTED STREAM, . . . THE PIECES OF APPARATUS I CONCEIVED WERE TO ME ABSOLUTELY REAL AND TANGIBLE IN EVERY DETAIL . . . WHEN NATURAL INCLINATION DEVELOPS INTO A PASSIONATE DESIRE, ONE ADVANCES TOWARD HIS GOAL IN SEVEN-LEAGUE BOOTS.

NICOLA TESLA

Have students write five things they dislike about their own behaviors or bodies. Then let them know that they're going to do some special work with one of those feelings, so they should select the one they most want to change.

Turn off the fluorescent lights and begin with the relaxation ritual— straight spine, three fingers, comfortable body, deep breaths, go inside, relaxation session—as required to suit their needs. The key or seed words in this exercise and subsequent exercises are in bold type. When reading the story line, subtly emphasize these words in a manner most natural for you.

Now imagine that you are with a group of people who are all feeling the same way about themselves as you feel about yourself around that issue you have in mind . . . There you are . . . with all those others . . . feeling absolutely terrible . . . really getting into feeling bad . . . "Yes . . . you're right . . . that's the way you are" . . . feeling badly. (Pause.)

*Now . . . let yourself slowly begin to **move away** from that scene . . . You can find yourself **moving** right **away** from those others . . . **to** a different place . . . **a safe place** . . . where you can observe the others from a distance . . . while you **move** easily **to a new place** . . . at a distance from the others . . . so you can now tune in to how you **feel** . . . **being at a distance** from the others . . . and **not involved** with them . . .*

*And from your new place . . . you can begin to **think of an opposite feeling** . . . just think now, if **you** were **okay** . . . right **now** . . . the **way you** really **want to be** . . . how could you **feel?** . . . Here you are, **in a new place** now . . . and as if by magic, **changing yourself** into the person that you really want to be . . . just **let that happen** now . . . **Allow yourself to change.** (Pause.) And how are you now? . . . How are **you different?** . . . And what really good feelings can you have now with your new image? . . . the new you . . . **feeling good** all over with the new you . . . being **just the way you want to be** . . . and you can **feel good** about yourself as the new you . . .*

*And you might even **imagine** the **good** new **feelings** . . . filling you up . . . like a fountain filling with water . . . filling you up from feet to head (pause) and then that **good feeling** overflowing from the top of your head . . . overflowing everywhere (pause) flowing all the way to the group you left behind . . . and as those good feelings flow all around and splash all over that group . . . you can watch now how the looks on their faces can change . . . to smiles . . . and how those **smiles spread** to all of the group . . . until **they** can **feel great** too . . . just like **you** . . .*

*And now you can begin to move back to that group . . . because they are also feeling good about themselves, thanks to you . . . and **your** good feelings . . . and isn't it amazing . . . just how you can **let yourself feel** really **happy** . . . because in a moment I'll ask you to begin to count slowly from 1 to 5 . . . and return your awareness to this room as you take a deep breath and bring good feelings about yourself back to the room with you.*

THE HEALING PATH (AGES 7-14)

Turn off fluorescent lights and begin with the usual ritual: comfortable body, straight spine, three deep breaths, close eyes, go inside.

Explain the following to students.

You know that you have the power to talk with your physical body using mind videos, and you can do this to relax yourself any time you want to. You can use mind videos to improve in sports and in studying and make learning so much easier.

Do you know that you can learn to feel better using imagery? That you can affect your health? Today you will learn how to give your body suggestions to feel even better, to be even healthier than you are now.

You know how your heart pumps blood all over your body—in tiny tubes called blood vessels. The blood contains both red cells and white cells, and they do different kinds of work to keep you alive and healthy. The white blood cells have the job of defending your body by destroying invaders such as bacteria and viruses that carry disease.

*Imagine now that your white blood cells are like dots of lights . . . very tiny and very powerful . . . and you have millions and millions of these tiny dots swimming around in your bloodstream . . . always on patrol . . . 24 hours a day . . . ready to **attack** and **destroy** any **invaders** that might get into your body . . . **keeping** your **body healthy** . . . and you can perhaps feel what it's like to have millions of tiny, powerful dots of light in your blood . . . moving all the time . . . and now feel those dots of light begin to shine even brighter . . . becoming so bright that your blood vessels seem to be lit up with light . . . from the millions of tiny, powerful dots of light inside your blood vessels . . . and the light can become so strong that it begins to **light up** the inside of your **body** . . . all over . . . so that your entire **body** begins to be **alive** with a warm glow of light all over . . . as you begin to **fill** with that wonderful **light** . . . you can let that **light focus** on any part of your body that needs some attention . . .*

*So **be aware** now of what bothers you in your body . . . and what needs **fixing** and can you **find** that **place** . . . that wants to **feel better?** because you can let your inner **light go to that place** . . . because the light **knows what to do** . . . and you can just **watch** it . . . and **feel** it . . . so that your body **glows with** wonderful **light** . . . all over . . . and you can **imagine your body** . . . **perfect** . . . just the way you **want it to be** . . . and **glowing with light** . . . **feeling good** in your body . . . and **feeling strong** . . . and able to **do whatever you want to do.** (Pause.) Can you feel yourself in your body **feeling** very **good** all over? . . . because you **can** do that . . . and you can take a minute of clock time, equal to all the inner time you will need to allow yourself to see yourself **glowing with light** in your perfect body . . . feeling healthy and able to **do whatever you wish to do** . . . very **well.** (Pause for two minutes.)*

*In a moment, I'll count from 1 to 5 and you can count silently along with me . . . and when you reach 5 you can still **feel** very **good** . . . and **strong** . . . and **alive** all over . . . as you let your eyes flutter open and return your awareness to the room . . . refreshed and ready for our next activity.*

SUGGESTION IS EVERYTHING AND EVERYTHING IS SUGGESTION . . . IN FACT, YOU CANNOT NOT SUGGEST. THE QUESTION IS, "WHAT ARE YOU SUGGESTING?"

ERIC JENSEN

SUCCESSFUL EXAM WRITING: SUGGESTIONS TO TEACHERS

1. Use the same special classical music selections for study periods and test-taking periods. Encourage the students to use the same selections whenever they study so that the music will help them access their memory for the correct answers. The music should be soothing, quiet, slow (about one beat per second), and without strong rhythms. (See the appendix for suggestions.) Slow, calm music helps slow students' brain waves into the

OUR PHYSICAL SCIENCE DOES
NOT NECESSARILY DEAL WITH
REALITY, WHATEVER THAT IS.
RATHER, IT HAS MERELY
GENERATED A SET OF . . .
RELATIONSHIPS TO EXPLAIN
OUR COMMON GROUND OF
EXPERIENCE . . . WE HAVE
DEVELOPED MATHEMATICAL
LAWS BASED . . . ON A SET OF
DEFINITIONS OF MASS, CHARGE,
SPACE AND TIME . . . WE DON'T
REALLY KNOW WHAT THESE
QUANTITIES ARE . . . BUT WE
HAVE DEFINED THEM TO HAVE
CERTAIN UNCHANGING
PROPERTIES . . . WE APPEAR TO
BE ENTERING A PERIOD OF
HUMAN DEVELOPMENT IN WHICH
CERTAIN QUALITIES OF THE
HUMAN BEING APPEAR TO BE
ABLE TO CHANGE . . . THESE
BASIC QUANTITIES. THUS, OUR
SET OF LAWS OR CONSISTENCY
RELATIONSHIPS WILL HAVE TO
CHANGE TO EMBRACE THIS NEW
EXPERIENCE.

WILLIAM TILLER

alpha range, where absorption and recall of information is best accomplished.

2. Have good ventilation and fresh air in the examination room, if possible. Encourage students to breathe deeply and fully to reduce stress. If the room does not have windows that open, use several air ionizers, and hope for the best.

3. Fluorescent lights are *not* conducive to generating slower alpha brain patterns and thus are *not* conducive to learning. The rapid pulsations of fluorescent bulbs tend to pace the brain into its fastest channel, Channel 1, which is not our learning mode. Fluorescent lights should be installed so that the light bounces off the ceiling or walls rather than beaming directly down. Use natural daylight or incandescent lighting as frequently as possible during both learning and examination sessions. (See Ott 1985).

4. Use guided imagery for good recall and a relaxation exercise for one or two days before exams and again before handing out exam papers.

5. During the exam, remind students to take deep breaths. Every five minutes or so simply say, "Breathe." The reminder will help reduce stress and slow brain waves.

6. Suggest to students that they first scan the exam, noting the types of questions and holding the image in their minds of being able to come up with answers readily and easily. Suggest also that they skip over any question they cannot answer readily and come back to them later—giving the brain a chance to search its memory banks for the answer.

7. Avoid grading on a curve. Reward good performance, striving for all to receive A grades. If we wish to encourage excellence in learning, we must remove our restrictions on it. A "Gaussian" or "bell" curve is the *result* of performance over a large, random group of humans, animals, plants, and so on. The concept of the curve was *never* meant to be *imposed* on a set of data. Such an imposition is neither scientifically accurate, morally fair, nor educationally smart. It forces some to fail who are just the ones who badly need to succeed, and who *can* indeed succeed in teacher terms, if graded on percentile brackets (90 to 100 percent = A) or another such open system. It is time we helped every student be a winner rather than condemning some to be losers. It is the classroom experience that helps label children as losers so long as *failure* is an operative word in the schooling system.

8. Encourage students to use their preferred learning mode when scanning the memory for answers to questions (that is, to *see* pictures, *talk* to themselves, or get a *feel* for the right answer).

9. Always return exams to students, allowing time for reviewing of *correct* answers so that students will not be anchored into incorrect responses. It is best for students to leave a review with images of correct answers in their minds. Thus they can associate with the correct answers and with feeling successful. Do you recall occasions in your life when you were not given the correct answers or the correct ways to do something and were left to operate without a standard to perform to? How did it feel? Is not the same principle involved here?

10. Think back to when you were a student taking exams. What might have been done to make your task easier and perhaps more successful? What else might you do to help your students be successful performers?

HUMAN BEINGS, BY CHANGING THE INNER ATTITUDES OF THEIR MINDS, CAN CHANGE THE OUTER ASPECTS OF THEIR LIVES.

WILLIAM JAMES

WRITING YOUR OWN SCRIPTS AND STORY LINES

Here are lists of possible topics you can use as metaphors to create your own scripts. With a metaphor, a message, and some inspiration, you're on your way!

Crystal Cave
Enchanted Forest
Magic Mountain
Quiet Pond
Dewdrops Dripping from a Leaf
Wafting Breezes
Wind in the Trees
Heartbeat
Magic Carpet
Rainbow Bridge
Your Personal Cloud
Protective Bubble
If You Had X-Ray Eyes

Flying Horse
Quiet Stream
Under the Sea
Sliding down a Slide
Sliding down a Tunnel
Moving through a Breeze
Watching a Candle
Be the Wind
Be the Mountain
Be the Animal
Warm Spa Bath
Immersed in Color

11

MATH, SCIENCE, AND BEYOND: SUBJECT-SPECIFIC EXERCISES

You can use directed imagery and Positive Outcome Patterning to facilitate students' success in specific subject areas and classroom programs. Once you've had some successful experiences facilitating directed imagery, you'll probably want to create your own story lines or adapt those from the book to fit your students' needs. The Positive Future Balloon exercise is a good general approach to success that can be adapted to any situation. Following that you will find examples of scripts that you can use in physical education, math, and science.

POSITIVE FUTURE BALLOON (AGES 12 TO ADULT)

This exercise reminds us of the power of our thoughts to shape and color our future experiences. One of the habits we tend to develop is to allow ourselves to image what we want but then imagine a zillion reasons why we will not be able to achieve it. As experience tends to follow thought, we sure enough do not get what we wanted.

WHAT CAN WE DO?

We seem to have an inner comfort range, which permits us to have this much, but not that much, of success, achievements, good health, close friendships, and so on. What can we do when our desires exceed what we believe we deserve? First we will want to explore how we can expand our comfort range to allow ourselves to have and enjoy more of the good things in life. We need to give ourselves inner permission to have a better life. As the inner permission develops, it will be reflected in outer experiences.

The Positive Future Balloon exercise can be of help in several ways. First, it keeps us focused on success rather than on failure. Second, when doing the exercise, we send a message to the brain's powerful Pattern Maker that it is okay for us to have that which we want. Third, it sends a message to our brains to get to work on attracting us to the experience of achieving what we want.

Here are some sample instructions to students that you can put in your own words:

It's a good idea to set goals for ourselves, for things we'd like to do or have, or achieve in the next few weeks and the next few months. You may want to be a better athlete or be more popular, or you may need a certain amount of money for a special project. I know there are goals you can think of that could make your life better. (Pause.)

Today we will explore how to set goals and a very interesting way to help make them come true. In a few moments, I'll ask you to begin a list of some goals that are important to you. Put on your list one goal that you would like to achieve in the next week. Add another goal that you would like to achieve in the next couple of months. Then write a goal that you would like to reach within a year. On the top of your paper write:

WHAT I REALLY WANT TO DO (or HAVE or BE)

1. in the next few weeks
2. in the next few months
3. in the next year

Here are some things other students have written:

to feel better about myself

to have people like me

to lose 5 pounds

to do better in school

to be a star player in my favorite sport

to get along better with _____

to have a healthy body

to sing very well

to play the guitar very well

to have confidence that I can do whatever I set my mind to

to look great when I go out on a date

to get a good job

A HUNCH IS CREATIVITY
TRYING TO TELL YOU SOMETHING.

FRANK CAPRA

Now that you all have three goals that are important to you, we'll do an exercise to keep you focused on achieving your goals. By keeping your thoughts on your goals, you can help yourself to get there. And would you like to know the secret of getting there?

*Part of your brain is in charge of future planning. You can learn to talk to that part and learn how to put in an order. The Future Planning Department doesn't take orders that come in words, but it does take orders that come in **images,** or **mind videos.***

So if you create a mind video, as if it were really happening right now, that will be a clear order to the Future Planning Department for what you would like to be or have for yourself. And I know that when you create a mind video of what you really want, you might surprise yourself by discovering what you can do to get it. So let's get ready to go inside and imagine enjoying the goal you have listed first on your sheet.

. . . now I don't want you to get your body too comfortable . . . until you take 3 long breaths . . . deep breaths . . . breathing in a warm light . . . and as you breathe out, you can let your body find that wonderful comfortable place even more . . . and as you breathe in light . . . you can let that light fill you . . . then breathe out again . . . and note how good that feels.

Good . . . now begin to imagine yourself already having your first goal . . . living it . . . enjoying it as if it were happening right now . . . so that you can see yourself doing it (pause) and feel how good that is (pause) how good it is . . . living your first goal . . . Take 2 minutes of clock time . . . which will be equal to all the inner time you will need . . . to fully enjoy living your goal . . . do that . . . now . . .

If students have listed goals that they feel comfortable sharing, you can follow the imagery session with small groups (2 or 3 people). Students should tell others their imagery using first person narratives (e.g., "I am out on the ball field . . .").

Have one person serve as monitor to keep the speaker in the *first person.* You might wish to demonstrate with an image/goal of your own.

Repeat the exercise to include the other two goals. Follow up with whatever discussion or activity you deem appropriate.

CENTERING IN PHYSICAL EDUCATION

A sizeable body of research shows us that mental practice in many areas of physical activity can successfully augment physical practice. When relaxation centering training is combined with mental practice, improvement in performance can be dramatic. Olympic athletes of most nations are currently being coached with this strategy, and you can use it effectively with your students. The process is called *body/mind patterning.*

It works quite simply: First, students are instructed in centering and relaxation. Then the athletic routine is imagined as vividly as possible, first by watching an imagined model, then by imagining being in that model's body going through the exercise. Here is an example from a coaching session with beginning tennis players. The students are sitting or lying on the floor, eyes closed, and relaxed.

Picture the tennis pro, serving the ball in slow motion . . . Watch him throw the ball into the air . . . noting his body stretch, arm reaching up with the racket . . . See how his eyes stay fixed on the ball . . . Now watch as he connects with the ball, hitting it perfectly into the opponent's court. (Pause.) Now feel your racket in your own hand . . . and note how you grip the racket . . . Feel how perfectly balanced it is, like an extension of your arm . . . Now feel the ball in your other hand . . . Feel yourself balanced and poised . . . Now imagine tossing the ball into the air, in slow motion . . . Your body stretches, your racket arm moves, and you connect, sending the ball perfectly into the opponent's court.

An Israeli physicist, Moshe Feldenkrais, has developed more than 2000 mind image exercises to help those who have lost some or all motor ability in their limbs to make significant and seemingly miraculous recoveries. We actually use this process unconsciously every day as we chatter to ourselves, in our head, telling ourselves how we can or cannot do things, and how successful or unsuccessful we will be in upcoming events.

Thus, using this process with a focus on positive outcomes, we can improve body awareness and performance. The same skills that can be used in the classroom to help students maximize the joy of learning can be used in physical education to teach and celebrate the joy of body movement.

As you work with students, follow these steps:

1. Teach centering/relaxation.
2. Follow with walking from our center point.
3. Select a sequence of movements that students wish to improve, and guide them in a slow motion imagery/fantasy exercise that covers each movement, describing how it is to be performed to perfection. If students can identify with a model, have them first imagine the model performing. Then have them put themselves in the picture, jump into the model's body, and perform just as well.

MASTER TEACHER EXERCISE (AGES 7-16)

In this exercise we again invoke the aid of a helper, who represents our own greater capabilities. If we simply told ourselves "perform better," we would be talking to Channel 1, which does not know how to perform any better by itself than at its present level. If we use an image, however, we are communicating with and calling into play Channels 3 and 4 and are better able to mobilize the brain's unlimited resources to help us create a new pattern to perform at new and higher levels of accomplishment.

Begin the exercise with a relaxation ritual: comfortable body, straight spine, three deep breaths, go inside . . .

THE REAL VOYAGE OF DISCOVERY CONSISTS NOT IN SEEKING NEW LANDSCAPES, BUT IN HAVING NEW EYES.

MARCEL PROUST

. . . now imagine that you have been chosen to attend a special training camp for your sport . . . a wonderful place for people really keen on improving their performance . . . a place you get to go for several weeks to work with master coaches who are there to give you personal attention . . . so you can learn to play your sport much better than you do now (pause) and you can take yourself to that special sport training camp. (Pause.) It's a beautiful warm day and there you are . . . at the camp . . . arriving with a small group of other athletes . . . and feeling very good about having been selected to come here to improve your game . . . and have a great time doing it . . .

So take a look around now . . . Over there is a large building . . . a dining hall where everyone gets together for meals . . . . and another large building with a big fireplace . . . for gathering around the fire at night after dinner . . . to sing and play and enjoy one another's company . . . and perhaps to watch videos of great athletes performing in your sport . . . and way off over there are the cabins where you and the other athletes will sleep and shower . . . and put your personal gear. Each cabin has 4 sleeping rooms . . . and you get to choose one for yourself . . . and each cabin has a porch . . . or veranda . . . to sit and talk about how you are doing and how the play is going with your coach helping you. (Pause.) And off in the other direction are the playing areas . . . where you can practice. (Pause.) So take a good look around; at the green grass and all the large trees and the flowers . . . and let yourself feel really pleased to be here at Training Camp . . . . because in a few minutes . . . you will meet your master coach and go out on the field for your first warm-up lesson . . .

So off to your cabin now . . . and gear up. (Pause.) Good . . . and now off you go to the practice field; along with the other athletes (pause) and here comes your coach now . . . with a big smile and a handshake for you . . . as you both say hello . . . and walk over to the practice area . . . and you can feel just how good it is to know that you are with someone who really cares about you . . . and who knows you very well . . . and you can listen as your coach explains how you will go through all the movements you do in your sport . . . and then your coach will demonstrate them in smaller bits . . . so that you can work on improving a few movements at a time . . .

So now, what is the first series of movements you make in your sport? (Pause.) Because in a moment . . . your coach will demonstrate just how it is to be done . . . and you can watch the demonstration in s-l-o-w—m-o-t-i-o-n (draw out words slowly) . . . so that you can get every movement perfectly in your mind . . . so let's do that now . . . Take 1 minute of clock time, which will be equal to all the inner time you need . . . to watch your coach go through the first set of movements in slow motion . . . perfectly . . . and you can learn from that . . . now. (Pause for 1 minute.)

Good . . . now in a moment you will get to do that . . . and very well too; so imagine now that there you are . . . ready to go through those same motions yourself . . . and feeling great and confident; and we'll take another 2 minutes of clock time, equal to all the inner time you need . . . for you to feel yourself in your body, and going through each motion . . . in slow motion . . . just like your coach did . . . easily and very well, and do it all several times and let's do that now. (Pause for 2 minutes.)

Good . . . and you can learn with this way . . . and have a lot of fun.

At this point you could have students recall the next segment of movements, simply repeating the coaching demonstration and the student practice sequence for the second segment. Alternatively, you might have students return their focus to the classroom and comment on their imagery experience. Some students might be successful with the imagery but not allow themselves to perform well. Knowing this can help you identify those who might benefit from "Let it be okay to succeed" scripts. Remind students that they are not to watch a video of themselves from a distance going through the exercises, but to imagine actually being in their bodies, doing the exercises. When we run mind videos of ourselves being successful and having fun, we want to make the imagery experience as real as possible for the best effect.

This is a marvelous use of imagery for practicing and improving all athletic performance. You can even test it: Divide your students into two groups. Have one group practice free throws on the basketball court while the other group practices free throws in their minds. Then take them all out to the court and collect your own statistics.

Science Lesson: Plant Projection Exercise

The brain exhibits a variety of "special" abilities that, when encouraged in the early years, can play a significant role throughout life. One example is the ability to project awareness into another energy system or material form, such as a plant or animal, and to sense information about the system. (Our "warm-up" exercise, "See your partner as _____" can at times elicit such ability in some students.)

We possess this ability innately. People who attain high levels of success in their work often attest to this ability, referring to it as an inner knowing, intuitive sense, gut feeling, or simply knowing.

This exercise invites students to focus awareness into a plant. You might use it both before and after the study of plant structure and physiology to help reinforce the learning process. If you redesign the exercise to be an anatomically/physiologically correct guided trip through a plant, you can additionally provide students with a *multisensory learning experience designed to enhance information up-take and ease a future recall.*

Some students may demonstrate an ability to accurately sense plant features prior to taking in information in the conventional way. This intuitive phenomenon is natural and can be exciting for students to discover and practice. Be noncritically responsive to validate students' processes of discovery, as well as to encourage others to allow the awakening of their expanded brain function. Thus you can encourage building self-esteem while facilitating whole-brain accessing and hemispheric integration.

Begin with a ritual for relaxation.

Good . . . and how easy it can be to go inside . . . to allow your body to be calm . . . and to feel that delightful pleasure that comes with inner calm . . . as you become aware of how you are breathing . . . steadily . . . in and out. . . watching how your breath comes in . . . and how easily it goes out . . . and you can notice how your body simply lets go and relaxes . . . relaxes more and more . . . while you tell your thoughts to . . . be still . . . be still . . . and note how good that can feel . . .

. . . because now I invite you to imagine that you can work magic . . . and change your body size . . . imagining now that you can shrink in size . . . and become smaller . . . and it's quite easy, safe, and fun, actually . . . to imagine becoming smaller . . . and becoming smaller now . . . down to four feet tall . . . and down to three feet tall . . . allowing yourself to be aware of how interesting that feels . . . to be three feet tall . . . while you can shrink even more. . . down to two feet and one foot tall . . . just like Alice did in Alice in Wonderland . . .

. . . and becoming so tiny that you can fit easily into a drop of water . . . keeping a bubble of air around you . . . safe and comfortable in your drop of water . . . you can slip into the soil around the plant . . . and have the delightful experience of moving down through the soil . . . down to the roots of the plant . . . cool and nice . . . in your bubble of water . . . coming to rest on a bit of root . . . and you might want to take a moment now to feel the moist soil and note its pleasant, sweet smell . . . and listen for sounds around you (pause) and be aware of what you see around you . . .

. . . because now you can be drawn up into the root, with anticipation of discovering how the plant food and water move along the root up into the plant . . . safe inside your bubble of water . . . looking out at how the plant works and that you are inside the root . . . all the while being carried gently up as the plant moves water and food up the roots . . . and into the large main stem . . . carried upward . . . streaming along (pause . . . and what do you see from your bubble? (pause) and are there interesting aromas to sniff? . . . and what sounds can you hear? as you move up the large stem. . . and here we come to a place where the big stem branches into a smaller stem . . . and the smaller stem has leaves at the end . . . and moving now into that smaller stem . . . moving along in your bubble of water in the stem, to the first leaf . . . and following along the tiny leaf stem now as you might wonder what it would feel like to be inside a leaf . . .

. . . and as you wonder, your bubble of water carries you delightfully along and into the leaf . . . and can you see how the light changes? . . . as you flow along the veins of the leaf . . . and you might want to notice very carefully now how the light looks as it filters into the leaf. . . and how the water and food move along the veins of the leaf to feed and nurture it . . . while you enjoy your ride . . . and the sunlight . . . being so small and being able to be aware of all that is happening in the leaf . . .

And what sounds can you hear? (Pause.) And what nice feelings do you have? (Pause.) safe in your bubble of water now . . . as you move along and out to the edge of the leaf, where you can easily slip out and on to the outside surface of the leaf . . . and enjoy the warm sunny weather . . . exploring the outer surface of the leaf now . . . and what does it look like, sitting in your bubble on the leaf (pause) and knowing that when you have finished your exploring . . . you are very light . . . and can jump off the leaf and float pleasantly and safely to the ground . . .

. . . landing very gently in your bubble . . . and then taking a look all the way up to the top of the plant . . . from your place on the ground . . . to see and feel what that is like to be so small and looking up at a plant that is so large (pause) taking one final look . . .

. . . because now you are beginning to grow again . . . getting larger . . . coming out of your bubble . . . and growing up to one foot . . . and two feet . . . then three feet . . . and four . . . and right back up to your normal height . . . feeling wonderful and full of good energy . . . with new learnings that your creative brain can use to build new understandings . . . new knowing that can be translated into useful behavior . . . appropriate to your living needs . . . creating all the while in its wisdom, for your great benefit and growth . . . knowing that your creative brain can do all of that for you . . .

AND THE WORLD CANNOT BE DISCOVERED BY A JOURNEY OF MILES, NO MATTER HOW LONG, BUT ONLY BY A SPIRITUAL JOURNEY, A JOURNEY OF ONE INCH, VERY ARDUOUS AND HUMBLING AND JOYFUL, BY WHICH WE ARRIVE AT THE GROUND AT OUR FEET, AND LEARN TO BE AT HOME.

WENDELL BERRY

. . . because in a moment, I will count slowly to ten . . . and you can begin to bring yourself back to the classroom (pause) moving your fingers and toes . . . and feeling good in your body . . . as you bring your attention slowly back to the room . . . and when you're ready, take a deep breath . . . and open your eyes.

MATH IMAGERY EXERCISE (AGES 7 TO 10)

Begin with the usual routine: comfortable body, straight spine, three deep breaths, close eyes, go inside.

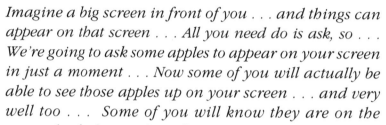

Imagine a big screen in front of you . . . and things can appear on that screen . . . All you need do is ask, so . . . We're going to ask some apples to appear on your screen in just a moment . . . Now some of you will actually be able to see those apples up on your screen . . . and very well too . . . Some of you will know they are on the screen by feeling or by talking to yourself, and that's good, too . . . Just take what comes to you . . . We're just going to play with images for a few minutes . . .

Okay . . . now put one apple up on your screen . . . and note what color it is . . . and how large it is . . . and if it has a stem or not . . .

Okay . . . now put 2 apples on your screen . . . Good. Now put 3 apples up there, and now 4 apples . . . put 4 apples on your screen.

Okay . . . let that image go . . . just let it fade. How were your apples arranged? . . . Were they in a straight line? . . . Okay. Next time, we'll put apples up on the screen and arrange them in a circle . . .

Now put one apple on your screen . . . now 2 . . . now 3 . . . Start to make a circle out of them . . . now 4 . . . and now 5 . . . arranged in a circle . . . 5 apples in a circle . . . Good, now let that image fade . . .

And now put 3 apples on your screen in the shape of a triangle . . . Got that? Good . . . Now open up the triangle to make room for another apple . . . 4 apples that change the triangle into a square. Make a square . . . an apple in each corner . . . 4 apples in the shape of a square . . . Good . . . Now see if you can open up the square and put in a fifth apple . . . to make a 5-sided figure—a pentagon . . . Can you do that? Okay . . . now let all of that fade . . . as I count from 1 to 5 . . . Slowly return your awareness to the room and we'll talk about how it was for you to imagine the apples on your screen.

12

SPEAKING TO THE WHOLE BRAIN: HINTS AND HOW-TO'S FOR FACILITATING

LANGUAGE PATTERNS AND DESIGNING STORY LINES

One of the fun and satisfying benefits of introducing yourself to brain-friendly tools is an increasing awareness of how you can use language to invite others to respond in ways useful to their growth and development. This statement may seem obvious as we use language every day to accomplish just that, but it is our hope and expectation that you will be pleasantly surprised with how much more aware and sophisticated you can become in your use of language to facilitate student growth.

This chapter presents advanced material. It will best serve those of you who discover a joy and challenge in encouraging and directly facilitating students to explore the further reaches of their potential. You can delight in becoming adept in using subtle language structures to further enhance this exploration. You can be an elegant facilitator of your students' high potential even if you completely ignore this short chapter and allow your own creative intuitive facilities to guide you.

Following are some interesting possibilities for your own creative brain to explore. By building these language structures into your scripts, you will be able to encourage students to speak more effectively to their brains' Learning and Pattern-Maker Channels.

NOMINALIZATIONS

If the word is a noun and you can't put it in a wheelbarrow, it's a nominalization, for example, *fulfillment, satisfaction, health, joy, success, balance, competence*. Nominalizations also include phrases such as *meaningful behavior, effective curriculum,* and *basic values*. We can generally define what we mean by the words, but no two definitions are likely to be the same.

When we use nominalizations in story lines, we invite the listeners to bring their own meanings and relevance to the words, thereby accessing expanded brain functions. Here is an example from a classroom story line:

> *I know that you have something going on in your life right now that is a **problem** . . . one that you'd really like to solve. Now, I don't know just what that **problem** is . . . or just what **talent** and **ability** you have within you that you can use to solve this **problem** easily, but I do know that your **genius brain** can come up with the answers and bring them to you . . . and that you can ask for **help** and it can be there for you.*

UNSPECIFIED VERBS

The more artfully vague we are about linking the verb to sentence content, the more we invite listeners to access their expanded range of brain function. Examples of useful verbs include *solve, change, do, think, wonder, understand, experience, create, discover, know, see, hear, feel, find*. Following is an example from a story line:

> *In a few moments, we will **learn** how an atom is constructed. Now I know that you can learn to take real delight as you **discover** new understandings that can come surprisingly into your thoughts.*

UNSPECIFIED NOUNS

Again we are purposely vague, encouraging listeners to bring their own meaning, invoke their own creativity, and be in charge of their own thoughts. Examples include *people, feeling, ideas, thoughts, special place, comfort*. Following are examples from story lines:

> ***Students** can be relaxed and feel good.*
>
> *As you sit there, you can notice a **certain feeling** and a delightful **sense of comfort**.*

CREATING CONNECTIONS

We can utilize the strategy of linking ideas that can lead to useful and helpful outcomes. Thus, the facilitator begins with observations of what is already occurring and links those words with something we want to occur in the future. Following are two examples from story lines:

> *I know that when you imagine yourself running and allow images to come to you, you can imagine yourself running fast and easily.*

> *As you find that most comfortable place, your body can relax even more.*

NEGATION AND NEGATIVE REQUESTS

Some language patterns can result in the opposite of what we intend. Negations provide fascinating examples. Say, for example, that we instruct a student: "Don't do that again" or "Don't run across the street." The brain hears two messages from these statements: *Don't* and *Do*. Why is this?

We cannot construct *negative* images in our thoughts, only positive ones. Negation is a derived concept, symbolically represented in language, mathematics, and art, but not representable in imagery. For the brain to derive meaning from language, it must *represent* what is spoken. What happens for you if someone says: "Don't think of a shiny red apple!" Do you not immediately experience an image of the apple? When admonishing a youngster, "Don't run across the street," the child's brain will first create an image of running across the street. Following that, the *don't* will register.

Thus, by directing or inviting a person to avoid a particular behavior, using the negative *don't* actually confuses the brain. To improve our effectiveness, we should do the following instead:

1. State what we wish to happen in its positive form. Example: "Stay on the sidewalk," rather than "Don't run into the street." "Be careful climbing that tree," rather than "Be careful that you don't fall out of that tree."

2. Interestingly, we *can* utilize negative requests for useful purposes, when students are in their expanded brain states, by stating clearly what we want to occur and preceding the statement with a negative. Example: "I don't want you to totally relax until you can find that most comfortable place for your body." Or, using two negatives, subtly: "I don't know how you will find that most comfortable place for your body now, but don't totally relax until you easily find it." This verbiage serves to confuse and

boggle the rational, logical awareness. Getting Channel 1 out of the way helps the listener to access expanded Pattern-Maker awareness, where the suggestion is readily processed without confusion.

IMAGERY AS A LEAD-UP TO OTHER ACTIVITY

THE HUMAN MIND, ONCE STRETCHED TO A NEW IDEA, NEVER GOES BACK TO ITS ORIGINAL DIMENSIONS.

OLIVER WENDELL HOLMES

Sometimes students will wish to pursue imaging more deeply and extensively beyond classroom time. We know of several social clubs that have formed, with teachers serving as volunteer advisors. One of these "inner exploration" groups selects a new topic each meeting. These topics have included athletic improvement through image-rehearsal, using intuition to enhance game competition, creative writing, artistic creation, and playing musical instruments. Students in the group enjoyed serving as story line readers and even story line writers on a rotating basis in the group.

CHANGING THE PAST

On occasion, we may feel limited by events that happened long ago in our personal history. Unpleasant memories from childhood—of not being loved, or of being criticized or made to feel inadequate—can color our outlook and hamper our growth as successful, happy adults. Memories can have a strong and lasting effect.

Must these past hurtful and limiting memories continue to affect us throughout life? Is there a way of working with them to diminish their impact on our present and future? Might we, in fact, find a way of countering the negative effects of these powerful memories?

WHAT IS MEMORY?

In practical terms, it is a tiny closed-loop tape recording that tells our version of a story of an event in our life history. "Outer" events happened as worldly experiences. Our inner senses processed those events to create our personal history and recorded that personal history in memory banks as repeating tape loops.

If we all witnessed the same event, each of us would record it in a slightly different way, depending on our attitudes and inner belief systems, and on what our perceptual system was able to observe. Each tape loop is uniquely ours. No one would have recorded the historic event exactly as it occurred.

These observations can be very useful. If inner mind events create new tape loops, and further, if we tend to distort events as we put them into memory anyway, we might already have a perfectly useful way to counter the continuing effects of painful and limiting memories.

Although we cannot erase our memories, we can use our natural memory-creating processes (Pattern-Maker Channel) to offset the impact of existing negative tapes. We know that by focusing thoughts while in a slow brain-wave mode, we do in fact create new tape loops. So we can custom make new, positive memories that are the opposite of old, painful ones; reinforce them through repetitive imagery to give them impact; and begin to counter the negative effects of old limiting tapes.

"Changing the Past" is a method widely used by counselors utilizing neurolinguistic programming (N.L.P.), Gestalt therapy, psychosynthesis, and Transactional Analysis. It works.

How to Call on Your Neurologic Capabilities to Change the Past

When recalling a negative past experience, remember that by dwelling on it, holding a vivid image of it, while in a relaxed state, we are—so far as our brains are concerned—reliving that event. In so doing, we "cut the groove" of that event deeper into our memories. In other words, we give that thought more power to run our lives. What can we do?

1. Stop the negative-outcome video as soon as you recognize that you are running it in your thoughts. Imagine a large X scrawled over that negative-outcome scene.

2. Rerun the scenario until just where it is ready to turn negative or painful. At that point, change the video to one that is loving and supportive of you and gets you what you really want. At the end of the new video surround the scene with a glowing light, and allow yourself to feel loved, supported, and pleased.

3. As an alternative to step 2, run a completely new video on the same theme, making it entirely positive, loving, and supportive of you. Complete it in the same way you completed step 2.

13

GETTING REAL IN THE SCHOOLS

PROBLEM SOLVING IN THE CLASSROOM USING REAL-LIFE ISSUES

We tend to get ourselves stuck on occasion, with our personal life issues and challenges. And it's no wonder that we get stuck. The wonder is that we successfully manage as many life issues as we do. Why? Well when you think about it, when were we ever instructed in designing and testing strategies for effective problem solving?

Curriculum in traditional schooling has been typically oriented to amassing information unrelated to practical, everyday problem solving. Unless we grew up in a home where parents modeled successful problem-solving skills, we may not have learned effective strategies for tackling our life issues.

GETTING REAL—"SLICE OF LIFE LEARNING" TO THE RESCUE

The classroom *can* be an excellent base for authentic learning when its focus is on the acquisition of problem-solving skills. What is required, in part, is to allow for information to be taken in and applied within a real-world problem-solving context, where the problem or issue is of high relevance to the present interests and needs of the student. If we relate this process to significant themes, we have the makings of a learning place that mirrors life in our everyday world. Here we have a practical and useful life skills education.

The theme model itself will probably be familiar to you and perhaps is already in use in some form in your school. What we offer here is *challenge learning,* which puts true-to-life problem solving into the theme context, along with a highly effective goal-orienting skill, directed imagery. Let's look at how this works, beginning with theme selection.

One of the major learning inhibitors in traditional Western schooling is the lack of relevance to students' immediate life interests and needs. Theme teaching can, if managed properly, be a highly effective tool for reintroducing life-relevance to the curriculum. The key to managing properly is to *allow students to identify a subtheme* of a theme that is of high interest to them. Thus, in *challenge learning,* the major theme must inspire myriad subthemes of high relevance to the immediate personal needs and interests of students.

Some examples of major themes include the following:

Yesterday, Today, and Tomorrow
Shelter Design for Living and Learning
How We Govern Ourselves
Cooperation
Cycles of Life
Creating Something Original
Movement and Mobility

In the challenge learning model, theme selection is a group effort. Before the school year, one or more major themes are selected by the teaching faculty. A major theme might run for a month, a term, or a year. Generally, every class uses the same major theme for the agreed-upon period.

Teachers also generate a long list of subthemes and bring this list into their classrooms. Students and parents give their input, and students identify a subtheme of high personal interest and relevance. The teacher helps students to identify further their Challenge Issue (real problem) within their subtheme context, which will be the focus for their classwork.

WHAT THE BEST AND WISEST PARENT WANTS FOR HIS OWN CHILD MUST BE WHAT THE COMMUNITY WANTS FOR ALL OF ITS CHILDREN. ANY OTHER IDEAL FOR OUR SCHOOLS IS NARROW AND UNLOVELY; ACTED UPON, IT DESTROYS OUR DEMOCRACY.

JOHN DEWEY

AN EXAMPLE

One successful use of the challenge learning model involved a high school faculty's selection of a year-long theme that was highly relevant to students, educators, administrators, and the local community. The community had passed a school bond issue to finance the construction of a new high school. The theme chosen by the faculty and administration was "Let's Design Our New School." Faculty and administration agreed that curriculum for the year was to derive from topics directly related to the design of the new school facility and, further, that the project was to reach into the greater community.

As the list of subthemes grew with input from parents and students, each student chose the subtheme that was of greatest personal interest. Working alone or cooperatively, with the help of classroom educators, students then framed subthemes into statements of real problems, which included the following selections:

THINK OF THE RISK-TAKING
IMPLICIT FOR KIDS JUST TO
GO TO SCHOOL. MAYBE IT'S
NOT SUCH A BAD THING TO
SEE THE TEACHER TAKING
RISKS, TOO.

PETER AMES RICHARDS

How could the overall site be planned for most effective land use?

What building shapes and configurations would be most effective as learning spaces?

How could the school building structures be integrated successfully into the natural environment?

What interior designs would be enhancing to the learning process?

How might traffic best flow within and around learning spaces?

What fabrics and colors would be most compatible with learning? What lighting has proven most conducive to learning, to physical activity, to assembly, to dining, to office and administrative work?

There were more than 150 others.

As students developed interest in real-life issues, the school administration kindled community interest for the project, which in turn generated mentor-partnership support from business and professional groups, who made time and resources available to students as an extended community resource base.

What happened in the school was magic. Students became intently focused and involved. Discipline problems virtually disappeared. School was real, a "slice of life."

The term began with lessons in effective communication, mutual problem-solving, and conflict resolution skills for all students to facilitate cooperative learning. A mini-course in mediation was offered for students who wished to learn to mediate disputes that might arise from team participation.

Students, with help from teachers, translated their chosen issues into step-by-step *strategic problem-solving sequences*. Students explored the following:

What precisely is our challenge?

What is the community resource base that we can access to provide us with information and skills we will need along the way?

How do we learn skills for effective communication with resource people?

How do we draft and type letters and send faxes?

How do we conduct successful personal interviews?

How do we gather data for future reference and processing?

What are the best ways to evaluate and process information to come up with working designs and solutions to our Challenge issue?

How do we select our best quality work for our individual portfolios?

What are effective ways to present our findings to the class, our teacher, and the larger community?

ADVANTAGES OF THE CHALLENGE MODEL

With the challenge learning model, curriculum content derives from life-relevant themes and is *learned as students encounter the need* for information and skills. The classroom facilitator may or may not be the provider of the data or skill training. Students might learn from personal research efforts, with peers in a team effort, from mentors in the larger community, from prepared lessons on videotape or audiotape, and so on. The classroom becomes a home base for coordinating the natural learning process, and the teacher is a guide and facilitator of the process.

The same elements that provide for superior learning in preschool years are present in this theme-based, problem-solving format. And with challenge learning, the learning process is returned to the learner. As in preschool, students can again more elegantly assume the role of creator, innovator, and designer and evaluator of the daily learning adventure.

With this model we can confront the basic questions for identifying and meeting educational standards:

What are life-essential skills worth mastering?

What constitutes quality performance?

How do we manage real world assessment?

Essential life skills define themselves daily as we dive into real issues. Quality performance is what learners are motivated to produce when the focus is on the excitement of authentic learning and on the developing of expanded-intelligence abilities.

When schools put learners into a challenging environment where they can feel excited, have an opportunity to be successful at whatever level they work, and are rewarded for stretching their limits rather than by standardized tests, their brains are motivated to push beyond learned limits. When our own performance as educators is judged, don't we clamor for just such a working environment, where we can do authentic work, teach to real-life issues, and be assessed for our excellence and the quality of our output? The challenge learning model engenders such an environment.

SCHEMATIC FOR "GREAT BRAIN" PROJECT

(THE GREAT BRAIN PROJECT IS A MODIFIED VERSION OF LYNN STODDARD'S (1992) IDEA).

Students arrive at classroom with conditioned mind patterns and stress

Calls for pre-lesson centering to ↓ decrease stress and ↑ increase focus

"GREAT BRAIN" PROJECT: TO BECOME SCHOOL EXPERT IN FOCUS AREA OF CHOICE

Phase 1:
Preparatory Phase
Pre-Lesson
Directed Imagery
to
↑ **body relaxation**
↑ **personal calm**
↓ **mind chatter**
↓ **personal stress**
↓ **class disruption**
(P.O.P. session 2)

Phase 2:
Teacher Introduction of Major Theme

Phase 3:
Positive Outcome Patterning 2
Scripting for success to identify quality of desired project outcomes

Phase 4:
Incubation Period
Time for superconscious mind to work at task creativity

Phase 5:
Inquiry-Centered Approach
Students choose focus area within theme and challenge context.

Phase 6:
Identify Resources and Generate Strategies
The who, what, why, when, where, and how of becoming an expert "Great Brain" in chosen focus area

Phase 7:
Teacher Lessons of Information and Skills
Teacher helps students identify "basket of tools" needed for project completion. These are put into lesson form to be taken on as needed during project.

Phase 8:
Develop Plan of Action
Deductive: from larger picture to sequenced steps. Individual assignments, timing of sequences, and checkpoints identified.

Phase 9:
Activation Phase of Plan

Phase 10:
Group and Individual Processing
of data and experiences to date

Phase 11:
P.O.P. Directed Imagery
(session 4: imaging successful presentation)

Phase 12:
Preparation of Presentation
by individuals and teams

Phase 13:
Presentation
to class, teacher, invited guests

Phase 14:
Personal Evaluation
and assessment of personal meaning and significance

Phase 15:
Follow-On Opportunity
for students wishing to continue with project activities as matter of personal interest

SLICE OF LIFE CURRICULUM

The diagram on page 124 provides an overview of a "slice of life" challenge learning model, which brings together components with proven success in the larger society of business, industry, recreation, sports, and medicine, as well as in school and non-school-based education at all levels. Following are more detailed comments about the various phases of this model.

PHASE 1: PREPARATORY PHASE

To enhance both new learning and extended performance, we begin all class sessions with a 3-minute Positive Outcome Patterning exercise for centering and calming, to facilitate students in making a transition from concerns outside the classroom to issues within the classroom.

Also called "Scripting for Success," the P.O.P. session is intended to help students first identify and then pursue goals of high interest. In our communication with Channel 4, we instruct the brain to create Positive Outcome Patterns, which it then runs through Channel 1. We thus introduce, at strategic junctions, educator-guided directed imagery, which encourages this intra-brain communication. This neurologically friendly method gets students on the way toward their goals by instructing the brain to activate its integrating processes in a particular direction. (The directed imagery exercises in this book are designed to help students and educators identify goals and achieve them.)

PHASE 2: IDENTIFY THE THEME

Using *multisensory* presentation, the teacher introduces a life-relevant *major theme* for the month, term, or year. The presentation, which should also include the faculty-generated list of subthemes, should be designed to stimulate interest, excitement, and anticipation in students. The idea to convey to the students is that this is an opportunity for them to find something that interests them strongly, something they would love to explore and get involved with.

The project gives them a chance to set challenges for themselves, figure out how to meet the challenges, evaluate their accomplishments, self-correct, and take the school term to do it. It's a chance for students to take charge of their own learning, a life-long skill.

PHASE 3: POSITIVE OUTCOME PATTERNING SESSION

Now is the time to encourage students to imagine how they might achieve some of their goals. We want to excite imaginations. The teacher can offer directed imagery as a vehicle for students to image their goals and make them their own. The story lines in this book provide you with a small library of imagery examples to use until you might feel ready to ad lib.

INTELLECTUAL INDEPENDENCE AT THE EARLIEST POSSIBLE AGE SHOULD BE THE OBJECTIVE OF EDUCATION. THE INITIATIVE SHOULD BE TRANSFERRED TO THE STUDENT AT THE EARLIEST PRACTICABLE STAGE. THE EDUCATION SHOULD HOIST THE CLIMBER UP FROM THE CHILD'S PASSIVE ROLE TO THE ADULT'S ACTIVE ONE.

ARNOLD TOYNBEE

In the diagram, the example major theme is the "Great Brain Project." The challenge is to become the school expert in the chosen subtheme. After guiding students into a relaxed-alert state, the teacher might construct a story line that goes something like this:

You might be wondering just how YOU might become a Great Brain . . . an expert in something of real interest to you . . . and wouldn't it be exciting to imagine yourself as an expert in something that you loved to do (pause) and to have other people know you as an expert . . . and listen to what you say (pause) and you might imagine now . . . how it would feel . . . knowing that you are a real expert . . . and feeling very confident that you could tell your friends and classmates about what you know and have them be interested to hear what you have to say (pause).

This story line uses process words, with no specific content at all. Thus, you can read it to thirty-five students, and each will bring to it her or his own personal images, vision, and goals, and incidentally, prepare nicely for the next active step of identifying their subtheme interest areas for the Great Brain Project.

PHASE 4: INCUBATION

As we know from our own natural habit of thinking about a problem, then letting it go and sleeping on it, the superconscious brain requires time to perform complex goal-seeking and problem-solving feats for us. Thus, when presented with a complex issue (such as the theme project and all its related activities), we should allow one or two days after a directed imagery session for the brain to process requests brought to it by the imagery and to set in motion its amazing functions on our behalf, in its seemingly effortless manner.

PHASE 5: SELECTING A SUBTHEME

Working with the list of subthemes generated by the school faculty, and possibly with parent participation, each student now identifies a personal subtheme. (Students might also add their own possibilities to the list.) In our example, students would select a subtheme of sufficient interest that they would be willing to become experts in areas of knowledge.

The theme identification is the first major *decision junction,* designed to help students successfully face, identify, and act on real decisions. Learners can work individually or in groups on their project tasks.

The classroom teacher works with students, individually and in groups, to put their themes into real-life challenges, issues, or problems, the solutions and resolutions of which will be the focus for the theme period. This phase prepares students for the Strategic Problem Solving format, used extensively in the adult world, in which, after identifying a life issue, we assess the resources available to us and use those resources to bring our challenge to a satisfactory resolution.

SELF-EDUCATION IS, I FIRMLY BELIEVE, THE ONLY EDUCATION THERE IS. THE ONLY FUNCTION OF A SCHOOL IS TO MAKE SELF-EDUCATION EASIER; FAILING THAT, IT DOES NOTHING.

ISAAC ASIMOV

PHASE 6: RESOURCE IDENTIFICATION AND STRATEGY GENERATION

In this phase, students learn to research and identify resources appropriate to their needs (for example, educators, publications, community agencies and professionals, local businesses, parents and relatives, peers). Students then explore and work out strategies for their project activities. They will also need to identify possible working constraints (transportation, expenses, time out of class, and so on). As students develop approaches to access their identified resource universe, they can begin to take on individual and team assignments.

This phase supports the development of cooperative skills, replacing the competitive model with the truer-to-life team model to facilitate *emotional* support for all learners. We want each learner to emerge from daily work feeling like a winner. The model generates the need for team members to support each other to ensure success for team-related activities. In this phase students can begin to develop skills in communication, cooperative learning, group decision making, conflict resolution, and mutual problem solving.

PHASE 7: ACTION PLAN

In this phase, students decide on ways to actively approach the project challenges. They explore *options* and *strategic planning* (involving higher-order thinking skills). All team members should feel that they have been heard. Encourage input from all members in an atmosphere conducive to *win/win* transactions. Use brainstorming to stimulate the flow of ideas after moving students into expanded brain states and imaging for success.

This phase calls for accessing and integrating fuller brain functions. Students begin with the overall theme (big picture) and, taking a deductive approach, identify smaller and smaller sequenced steps. These steps will include school-based and community-based information and skill uptake, individual and team assignments, and so on. At the completion of this phase, learners should know their tasks, understand the timing, have a good idea of what new information and skills are required, and feel ready to activate their plan.

PHASE 8: INSTRUCTION

For the balance of the project period, students will be learning relevant information and skills. The teacher works with each individual or group to help students identify what they need to learn and how to be successful.

As a facilitator, you have the opportunity to create relevant school-based instruction and to facilitate students' learning in the greater community. You also have the opportunity to work with small groups, individuals, and the whole class.

In this and subsequent phases, students can continue to develop effective social and communication skills, as well as skills in group decision making, conflict resolution, and mutual problem solving. (You can teach problem-solving skills yourself or bring in a consultant.) You have the opportunity to be a facilitator of the natural learning process (refer to chapter 3), a guide, a direction-pointer, a counselor, a communications consultant, and a confidant. This role can dramatically lower stress levels for both students and classroom educators and turn the classroom into a productive home base for learning.

This is a good time for you to build into lessons as many learning enhancers as possible (see chapter 3). Be sure to include abundant rewards along the way, opportunities for fun and humor, and periodic celebrations to build class spirit.

PHASE 9: ACTIVATION OF ACTION PLAN

This phase requires your careful monitoring, with regular check-up meetings with teams and individuals to assess student motivation, process, and progress. In this relatively open-ended inquiry model, learners work with a high degree of independence (as they will later in college and in the work force). You can enhance their work toward identified goals using short P.O.P. sessions at the start of each day or session. Have students draw up short-term action plans daily, as well as record summaries of their activities in personal journals.

This phase can be expected to consume close to half of the project time. It will call into play and bring to the surface both skills and difficulties for each student. It thus brings to light areas in which students are patterned for success and areas in which they are patterned for less-than-success, which become excellent opportunities for personal growth—academically, socially, emotionally, and spiritually. Use the P.O.P. sessions to help change negative outcome patterns to positive outcome patterns. Begin with the most readily demonstrated changes, such as with relaxation and stress release, and gradually move on to more complex repatterning using story lines in the book or creating your own.

PHASE 10: PROCESSING, SORTING, AND EVALUATING DATA

In this phase, students bring personal meaning to project activities, form observations, and make tentative conclusions. Our objectives for students are to do the following:

1. Develop skills for amassing, sorting, evaluating, and using data.
2. Cultivate skills for presenting findings to others.
3. Relate project activity to real-life interests and needs. This ability calls for skillful facilitation. With the use of discussions and directed imagery sessions, you can help students look for and find meaning and relevance in their daily activities. The inner work that is most helpful is repeated imaging around the thought "I experience success and satisfaction in my life." Directed imagery that invites each student to imagine feeling successful and satisfied, as if the feeling were happening right now, can provide the appropriate setting.

A sample story line might go something like this:

I invite you now to dip into your wonderful memory to a time when you felt marvelously successful (pause) very successful . . . and satisfied . . . and pleased to be YOU . . . and happy . . . being successful . . . and how does that feel to you? . . . And can you remember that experience and those feelings? (Pause for one minute.) And remember to remember that wonderful experience and to call on those feelings in the future when you want to remind yourself what it feels like to be successful and feel fulfilled . . . because your powerful brain can bring you more of those kinds of experiences . . . and each day for the next week, we'll take time for you to go back and recall those good feelings so that each time you do so, you can perhaps feel them even more strongly . . . how good it is to feel really satisfied and pleased to be you.

As you will note, this is another process story line, designed to be artfully vague so that each person hearing it, while in a relaxed-alert state, can bring unique meaning to the words. If you then follow this with a story line more specific to the activity to which you wish to have your students relate, you can help them build a powerful and effective bridge between a well-established memory of good feelings and the upcoming activity. A more specific story line might go something like this:

. . . and recalling well those wonderful feelings of satisfaction and pleasure . . . I invite you now to imagine a scene where you are interviewing a person important to you, to get information about your project . . . Now you can imagine being in a pleasant room with that person . . . both of you sitting in comfortable chairs and talking easily . . . and you are asking that person for answers that will be of real help to you with your project . . . You don't even have to know now what those questions might be, but just imagine that person speaking to you with a bright smile on his or her face, and very interested in what you are doing (pause) and you feeling relaxed . . . and confident . . . and very pleased (pause) very pleased with yourself and with how well the interview is going . . . smoothly and easily . . . smiling now . . . both of you . . . feeling very good . . . very good (pause).

4. Develop the skill of drawing interim conclusions and making periodic evaluations of quality of process and progress, leading to identified goals.

5. Develop the ability to self-select examples of personal work exhibiting high levels of achievement to add to a personal portfolio, which will be one of the evaluation elements to be assessed by the classroom educator.

6. Hold in awareness possibilities for a final presentation to class-mates, the teacher, and, possibly, invited guests.

This phase is important for intellectual, emotional, and higher self-growth and is frequently absent in traditional schooling. It brings to awareness and allows for the development of specific life skills necessary for feelings of success in the working world, which is project oriented.

PHASE 11: POSITIVE OUTCOME PATTERNING SESSIONS

As we have indicated, it is most productive to use short, frequent P.O.P. sessions prior to each day's or period's work. It is also helpful to wrap up each session with a forward-looking directed imagery session for the next segment of work. In principle, it is not unlike the traditional dressing room pep talk. The difference is that an exter-nally offered pep talk is not as powerful over time as encouraging the habit of a daily self-actioned pep talk.

Because students' final presentations will undoubtedly be of a com-plex nature and require considerable focus and creative effort, you will want to facilitate frequent P.O.P. sessions that anticipate successful completion of this task, with the student emerging from the experience feeling good, accomplished, and having given it her or his best effort.

PHASE 12: CREATING THE PRESENTATION

Early in the challenge learning project, the educator will want to decide with students whether to grade this activity or not. The question in part is, Would grading or not grading be more conducive to creativity, original thinking, invention, and joy of learning? There is a good case for both sides of the question, and several options come to mind:

1. Devise a mutual support system between teams and individuals that invites student evaluation of each other's work, citing primarily the positive points of each presentation, and do not have this phase be graded by the educator.

2. Invite both student evaluation and educator evaluation, again emphasizing the positive, strong points of each presentation.

3. Run all presentations as an end-of-term celebration, and do it just for the fun of it.

4. Some combination of the above or some other options may come to you from your and your students' creative brains.

In any case, having completed highly focused, carefully planned, and meaningful activities and new learnings, students should have much to share and show. Presentations can take any number of forms: written reports, original theatrical skits, dance expressions, musical compositions, mathematical creations, crafts, computer models, audio-visual shows, graphic displays, video interviews, newspapers or magazines, and so on. The presentations can be individual or group expressions, which can include humor, with encouragement to express it in an accomplished, artistic manner.

This phase presents a special opportunity for you to foster a classroom environment in which it is safe for students to take risks. Bringing original ideas into the world requires a state of confidence, a trust of all concerned in the process, and openness to the new. Thus the classroom environment can permit and encourage access to high creativity brain functioning (a Channel 4 feature). These enormous, perhaps limitless, creative faculties are seldom called into play in traditional schooling. By introducing the opportunity for the genius-level brain to offer its highly creative, intelligent, and original accomplishments in a safe setting without deprecating experiences, we serve the cause of human expansion and growth in an elegant manner.

Here is a sample P.O.P. session for helping students announce the next creative assignment to their superconscious brains, so that the creative juices can begin flowing. Introduce the session with the usual calming and centering exercises.

. . . and off you go to your Special Place . . . where you can go when you wish to be very creative . . . and when you want to be open to wonderful new ideas . . . ideas that can be very useful to you . . . because now you can find yourself there . . . in your Special Place (pause) and at your place where new ideas can come to you easily (pause) and just by telling your Genius Brain the topic . . . it can serve you in many ways with ideas that can amaze you . . . because your topic today is the presentation that you will create from what you have discovered in our Great Brain Project . . . and your interesting observations and experiences . . . and your Genius Brain knows very well that it can design fun ways for you to present your ideas to the class. (Pause for one minute.)

LEARNING VIA PROBLEM-SOLVING INQUIRY IS A SELF-EMPOWERING ACTIVITY. LEARNING IS MORE LIFE-SATISFYING AS WELL AS MORE EFFICIENT WHEN HONORED AS EMERGING FROM AN INNATE HUMAN DRIVE RATHER THAN PURVEYED BY OTHERS FROM WITHOUT.

GREGORY BATESON

And as your brain springs into action, it can be of real help to you (pause) as you can find yourself easily preparing your presentation either by yourself or with your team . . . whichever is the best for you . . . and in a few moments you will be invited to be in your Special Place and call on the help you need there to let ideas begin to come easily to you about how you will present your project findings to the class . . . confidently . . . knowing that you are doing it very well . . . because you ARE competent . . . and you know that when you are relaxed, your ideas can flow easily to you . . .

And now let's take 3 minutes of clock time . . . which can be equal to all the inner time you will need . . . to let ideas begin to flow to you . . . and come into your awareness . . . now or in the next few days . . . so let's do that now. (Pause for 3 minutes.)

Good . . . and you can allow yourself . . . to remain open to recall these new ideas . . . that may have come to you from your Genius Brain . . . so that you can write them down in a few minutes . . . and use the ideas to design your presentation . . . and have fun with it . . . because you CAN recall so well when you want to . . . and discover that you can use ideas from your Special Place . . . in ways that can surprise and please you . . . and now you can be ready to leave your Special Place . . . knowing how to return here . . . whenever you like . . . for more good ideas to come to you over the next days and weeks . . . just popping into your awareness at any time of the day or night . . . And whenever you are ready . . . allow the image of your Special Place to slowly fade . . . and you can feel good about what you have allowed yourself to do so well . . . because now you can slowly return your focus to this room . . . bringing good feelings back with you . . . feeling refreshed and ready to write or tape or draw or model your good ideas . . . so that you will remember them and can put them to good use. (Now bring student awareness back to room.)

Phase 13: Presentation

It is important for this phase to be fun and to encourage individual expression. It is a time for celebration, costumes, oratory, greasepaint, bravado, demonstrations, performances, wild applause . . . and more celebration, with many rewards. Building rewards into the system is an area of critical importance for our schooling systems. We still too frequently function with the cosmology that life is meant to be difficult, with its rewards few and off in the future. Successful human systems build significant rewards into each day.

Presentations provide wonderful opportunities for rewards on many levels to underscore the value of each individual, with open acceptance and support. (*Each individual* includes the educator, lest we forget.) This is a wonderful time for applause, acknowledgment, praise, and thanks from students, parents, and perhaps administrative faculty, as well as a good time for acknowledging the value of what has been learned and practiced!

In other words, this is a time for everyone to emerge feeling like a winner—which underscores the need to emphasize cooperative spirit rather than competition between students. With the cooperative model, everyone can be an "A" student. We are striving for excellence and personal growth, not statistics.

EVALUATION

Each student will perform in accordance with his or her internalized scripts, and the classroom educator needs to take such scripting into consideration—which makes the traditional grading system woefully obsolete, punitive, and exclusive. Is it not precisely the student with a terrible self-image who needs most desperately to feel like a winner in life? We need therefore to be able to evaluate performance in accordance with what that person will allow her- or himself to achieve. What revisions in our evaluation systems are needed for us to view student performance from this perspective?

The presentation can be a vital, emotionally moving, and image-changing experience for some students if it is cradled in a supportive, nurturing, cooperative, fun, and trusting environment. Part of our evaluation can be to note the level of risk taken, involvement of each student's multiple intelligences, original and creative thinking, personal stretch beyond the usually expressed limits, and other such considerations, which speak of our desire for each of our students to become more of who they can be.

PHASE 14: REFLECTION AND PERSONAL ASSESSMENT

Although we do not frequently include this phase in our schooling, it can be of profound, long-term benefit to learners of all ages. It involves open sharing in a *trust circle* of what the project meant to each individual. Here are a few questions that might elicit meaningful responses:

- ❋ What can you do now that you could not do before?

- ❋ What can you do better now than you could before?

- ❋ What tasks or challenges can you now face with more confidence?

- ❋ In what ways do you feel differently about yourself as a result of what you did or what happened during this project?

- ❋ What vignettes can you share that may communicate to others something significant to you that occurred as a result of project activities?

- ❈ What new communication skills (such as how to better resolve conflicts, differences, and arguments) did you learn?

- ❈ What did you learn about group decision making that might be helpful to you in the future?

- ❈ Did you make any new friends in the process of what we did?

- ❈ What does it mean to you to *learn* something?

- ❈ What did we do as educators and aides that helped you learn?

- ❈ What didn't work so well for you?

- ❈ With what did you have trouble?

- ❈ What would you like to do more of in the next project?

- ❈ What would you like to do less of?

- ❈ If you had to identify the greatest benefit or pleasure or new learning from this project, what might it be?

The Trust Circle is familiar in business and industry, thanks in great part to the work of the late William Deming. It is unfortunately rare for all but the youngest of learners in our schooling system to feel a sufficient sense of trust within the classroom setting to take the risks necessary to break out of pattern constraints and to test personal potential. We know how inhibiting peer constraints can be and how judgmental peers can be of one another.

Creating a safe and supportive atmosphere in the classroom is an art, and although highly desirable, may not be all educators' "cup of tea." It requires a clearly understood and accepted set of conditions for non-judgmental acceptance of all class members and of how they share their ideas and feelings.

One of our major objectives in this phase is to encourage, nurture, and validate the innate ability to bring personal meaning to life's activities and experiences. This ability is seriously missing in our society. Just as with a jigsaw puzzle, the individual pieces have no intrinsic value; their value is as part of a larger picture to which the learner is able to relate.

Your class lessons, for example, may be the best in town in all respects, but how your students eventually apply what they learn relates not only to their internal scripting, but also to how practiced they are in bringing meaning to pieces and events in the puzzle of life. Thus, it is important to assess classwork along with your students by asking "So what?" at the end of each project or lesson. Insofar as your classroom is an environment in which students take personal pride in bringing their best quality of performance and expression and are challenged to find meaning in that expression, the classroom becomes a safe place to do life's real work and a place to develop the art of finding personal meaning and fulfillment in our work. This is "slice of life" or "challenge" learning at its best.

You probably recall that special teacher who helped you change your life in some positive way. It is one of our dreams and objectives that more educators provide similar gifts to more students. For educators actively and consistently using theme and challenge learning and Positive Outcome Patterning approaches, such gifts can be more frequent in school-based learning environments.

PHASE 15: FOLLOW-ON OPPORTUNITY

Because challenge learning tends to attract high student interest and involvement, it is good for students to have the option to continue with advanced levels of project work, whenever it is practical to do so. Advanced-level opportunities can be highly rewarding on many levels. When involvement is based on interest, all students can have the opportunity to participate in a level of activities usually available only to the gifted learners.

EPILOGUE: LOOKING BACK AND LOOKING AHEAD

TALKS WITH TEACHERS

I sometimes refer to students as clients. Aren't they? If we were to view them as such, what might change in our daily approach?

If we put ourselves in the position of a client, and imagine enrolling in a formal life-skills school, what might we consider to be basic services due us? Well, we would certainly want to have a copy of the annotated course catalog, so as to know what mandatory and what optional courses were being offered. We would expect to tour the physical plant to get a feel for the quality of the buildings, comfort and configuration of the learning areas, and type and quality of learning hardware and software—expecting a good showing of state-of-the-art learning equipment and facilities.

We would have every right to inquire about the educational philosophy and approaches as well as the *research grounding* for what was taught and how it was presented, and we would expect the instructors to be knowledgeable and articulate in their responses.

Our bottom line expectation might very well be a curriculum based on skills immediately applicable to our real-world needs. Are there courses, for example, in effective communication skills, rapid reading skills, the art of effective brainstorming, mutual problem solving and conflict resolution, effective studying and test taking, accelerative learning? Is the environment safe and trustworthy so that students can regularly explore and discuss life issues of high priority to them?

Further, it would be relevant for us to ask how we would know when we had mastered the information and skills offered—in other words, how we would be expected to demonstrate mastery. How is assessment performed and by whom? Do school assessments parallel on-the-job assessment models? Are these performed once or twice a term, or are they ongoing? On what performance criteria are they based?

We would expect to be able to discuss the *learning methods* and approaches used in the school. Is information purveyed primarily via lectures, or are students involved experientially with what is to be learned? Are multiple intelligences addressed? How are students encouraged to identify and work in accordance with their individual learning styles? Is learning isolated or cooperative in the classroom setting? Is the classroom the only learning environment, or does the school involve the larger community in mentorship and hands-on learning, using the classroom as a home base?

In light of the above questions, which you might justifiably ask of a teaching institution, how is your school doing so far?

1. Are students advised in some detail as to what they will be expected to learn, why, and what course options they have?
2. Is your school state-of-the-art in terms of building design, lighting, air circulation, seating, floor and wall treatment, room configuration, computer learning equipment, recreation area and equipment, lounges, dining facilities, and so on?
3. How well prepared are your administrators (and you), to discuss the philosophic basis of your daily teaching methods and approaches? What research base can be cited to support your teaching methods? What could you cite right now?
4. Is your curriculum designed and operated on the basis of being immediately life-relevant to your clients? What information and skills can you expect to be pertinent and useful in their lives tomorrow? Next week?
5. How many times a month do you hold open-ended life issues discussions in an environment in which your clients have affirmed feeling safe and secure?
6. Is demonstration of mastery roughly equivalent to the style and form used in the real world? Where else in the world aside from school systems can your clients expect to be confronted with machine-scored exams and instruments that test only three of their intelligences (logical-mathematical, linguistic, and spatial)?
7. What learning approaches are available in your school system? Can clients learn individually or cooperatively? Is there a variety of seating, lighting, and sound/silent areas to accommodate individual learning styles? Do those who learn better in the afternoon or better in the morning have the opportunity to suit their needs? How are the needs of the tactile-kinesthetic learners met?
8. And finally, if your clients could choose to come to your school and to your classroom or to go elsewhere, how do you think the school and your services might be ranked?

I hope that you scored very well. These questions are presented for your own consideration, in a context of inquiry and self-evaluation.

Looking Ahead

The successful learner of tomorrow will be well versed in the arts of identifying worthwhile life challenges, holding visions for desired life outcomes, involving intuitive/creative faculties in the problem-solving process, identifying and accessing internal and external resources, learning needed skills and information efficiently via their Learning Channel, applying critical thinking to new learning, and bringing meaning to life through the entire process. Further, the successful learner will be skilled in *learning how to learn,* that is, being able to use skills and information better next month and next year than today. She or he will learn this skill by working with the Pattern Maker faculty to create new and powerful positive-outcome patterns that will drive behavior toward more and more success and life value.

As educators we have an exciting opportunity to bring magic into our learning and teaching environments—to tap into greatly expanded brain function, stimulate improved academic performance, facilitate personal growth at all levels, and promote superlearning within every child. We can embrace this opportunity by creating learning environments that support and encourage our natural and innate learning faculties.

I hope that my communication with you, via printed and spoken word, has highlighted the core factor for creating environments that foster expanded brain function, and has communicated the importance of this function in tapping the brain's great, and perhaps unlimited, potential for learning and performance. I also hope that your curiosity and motivation have been stimulated to pursue further your own expanded potential and to actively facilitate that pursuit with your students.

APPENDIX

The appendix contains a number of supplementary items to help you enhance your classroom and prepare it for brain-friendly learning. Item 1, the checklist, is for you to use on any day or after any teaching period as a self-evaluation. It will remind you of elements that you might want to work on or include in future lessons. Other items are instructions and tips to help you in your commitment to create an effective learning environment.

ITEM 1: TEACHER'S CHECKLIST FOR CREATING A BRAIN-FRIENDLY CLASSROOM LEARNING ENVIRONMENT

RATE EACH DAY:

0 = not possible   2 = little used

1 = not used, by choice   3 = much used

PHYSICAL ARRANGEMENTS/CONDITIONS IN CLASSROOM

_____   1. Comfortable temperature

_____   2. Fresh-air circulation

_____   3. Comfortable seating: chairs, cushions, carpet, and so on

_____   4. Lighting: natural incandescent, no fluorescent

_____   5. Sound: quality relaxation sounds; quality equipment

_____   6. Scents: pleasing, subdued aromas

EDUCATOR'S PRESENTATION

_____   7. Positive expectations for happy, useful outcomes

_____   8. Personal confidence to deliver excellent lesson

_____   9. Predelivery 30-second personal imagery session

_____   10. Acceptance of and respect for all student responses

_____   11. Awareness of voice/body congruent behavior

STORY LINE/SCRIPT

_____   12. Engages Channel 1 with interesting story line

_____   13. Speaks to Channels 1, 3, and 4 for positive, useful outcomes

_____   14. Flows easily with run-on sentences

_____   15. Uses language patterns to enhance communication with all channels

_____   16. Seeds specific P.O.P. suggestions

_____   17. Length of story is appropriate to age group

LEARNER PREPARATION

_____   18. Aware of potential benefits with use of imagery

_____   19. Participates voluntarily; other options available

_____   20. Body oxygenation via physical movement

_____   21. Brain oxygenation via several full breaths

_____   22. Crossover hemisphere-synchronization exercises (BrainGym)

_____   23. Comfortable body position; straight spine

FEEDBACK

_____   24. Session for student responses and experiences

_____   25. Acceptance of all responses; no value judgments

_____   26. Educator open to feedback suggestions

Date _____ Class _____

Group _____

Educator's Comments and Notes _____

_____

_____

_____

ITEM 2: EXERCISES FOR OXYGENATING BODY AND BRAIN

I have found two exercise/stretching series to be easy, fun, and successful in readying bodies for being quiet for a while. I recommend that you use either of these or another of your choosing before you begin classwork. Of course, check to make sure no one has an injury or another reason for abstaining.

EASY STRETCHING EXERCISES

Have students stand an arm's-spread length apart, with feet spread shoulder-width apart. All movements are to be done slowly and with breathing.

HEAD ROLLS

Begin with chin to chest. Roll head to one side, up, and around. (Do not drop head back.) Reverse. Do five head rolls in each direction. Breathing: Breathe in as head rolls up, out as head rolls down.

SIDE-TO-SIDE HEAD TURNS

Rotate head horizontally to one side, return to center, then rotate to other side (shake your head "no"). Breathing: Breathe in as you rotate to the side, out as you return to center.

ARM WINDMILLS

Place right foot forward, left foot back. Swing left arm in windmill fashion, full circle, beginning with ten full circles backward, followed by ten full circles forward. Reverse legs and arms. Breathing: Do circles slowly enough to permit taking one complete in-and-out breath. Initially, some younger children will want to speed up the circle movement. Allow them to do so, but gradually have them slow down their movements.

EASY TORSO TWISTS

Make sure there is sufficient room between students. Have them spread their feet a little farther apart than shoulder width. With elbows bent or with arms out straight, depending on room, twist torso to right, then left, repeating cycle fifteen times. Do ten to fifteen complete swings. Breathing: Breathe in as you rotate to one side, out as you rotate to other side.

HIP ROTATIONS

The objective is to rotate the hip girdle and lower spine. Begin with feet shoulder-width apart, hands on hips. Rotate just the hips to one side then the other. Movement should be from the hips down to the knees. Breathing: Breathe in as you rotate in one direction, out as you rotate in the other.

Advanced: If children are sufficiently loose and know how to keep a hula hoop rotating, this one is fun. The objective is to do a full circle with the hips, like a belly dancer. Again, the movement is from the hips down to the knees. Many older and less flexible children will move their entire bodies, without moving the lower back/hip region. This is okay; it just means they have lost important flexibility in their lower backs and may wish to practice this exercise to regain flexibility. Breathing: Breathe in for three rotations in one direction. Breathe out for the three rotations in the other direction.

Knee Rotations

This exercise is a good one for getting ready for the ski season or for in-line skating. With feet almost together, bend knees, hands on knees. Rotate both knees together in full circle, three in one direction and three in the other. Breathing: Breathe in for three rotations, out for the next three rotations.

Ankle Rotations

Place hands on hips. Balance on one foot while making circles with the foot and ankle. Reverse. Forget about a breathing rhythm for this one. If you have difficulty balancing, stop for a minute and do the following exercise: Imagine that one foot is going to become planted in the earth like a tree, with deep roots that will hold you in balance. Do the ankle rotation exercise after the imagery and note if children balance better.

Shake out hands and feet. Raise arms up and shake hands as if you were in a gospel revival meeting. Add any other finishing touches to the series, such as walking around and slapping hands (like "giving five" after a success).

Do-In Exercises

This series of exercises is a French version of an Oriental acupressure exercise. The object is to wake up the acupressure points on arms, legs, front of torso, and head, by gently slapping oneself. No need for detailed explanations, just that it is a "wake-up" series. The way it is done is always fun.

Each part of the exercise is done three times. Have children position their feet shoulder-width apart. Hold out the left arm horizontally in front. With right hand, slap left shoulder; continue slapping down arm to back of hand in a series of good slaps with a flexible right wrist. Repeat twice. Next, slap palm to armpit in the same manner. Repeat twice.

Reverse arms and repeat slapping routine for right arm.

Next, bring hands around to back and begin slapping your back as high up as possible, then slap down to hips and down backs of legs, continuing to front of legs, coming up legs, hips, and chest. Repeat twice.

Next, using fingertips or nails, whichever is preferred, tap head and face all over. Begin tapping at top of head at the center of the forehead, then tap along the center toward the back, to lower edge of skull at back of neck. Stop tapping and return to the forehead again, but with fingers out laterally a bit, tap once again from forehead to back of skull. Repeat with fingers out even farther. After doing this series three or four times, continue down side of head around ears, to cheekbones, from nose to ears, down cheeks, around lips and chin. Fingers should feel tingly. Shake out hands. Did you cover the entire head and face, excluding the eyes and nose? That's it!

ITEM 3: SUMMARY FOR FACILITATING OTHERS INTO EXPANDED BRAIN FUNCTION

- Body movement and oxygenation
- Comfortable body position
- Straight spine
- Touch thumbtip, index, and middle fingertips of one hand together
- Decrease 5-sense focus
- Take several full diaphragmatic breaths
- Increase inner focus
- Use directed imagery
- Expect positive results

WHAT DO I SAY? (MY SCRIPT)

Objective is to keep Channel 1 pleasantly occupied while speaking with Channels 3 and 4. Use prepared story line or make up your own.

HOW DO I SAY IT? (VOICE FACTORS)

Volume: Low; just loud enough so that all can hear without straining, but no louder.

Pitch: Use your lowest comfortable register, which will be most conducive to helping others move into expanded states.

Tone: Use *natural conversation* tones, as if you were carrying on a normal conversation. Avoid *teacher dialect* speaking.

Sonority: Imagine that you are speaking to a group of your best friends. Your voice will then be supportive and most sonorous.

Pace of Delivery: Slower than you would imagine to be appropriate. Check with students to verify most appropriate pace.

Highlighting of Key Words and Phrases: Find your own best way to do this. You might elongate a word, place greater emphasis on it, pause momentarily before or after saying it to underscore its importance. These important words are the *seed words* that are already in bold for you in some of the story lines.

HOW WILL I RECOGNIZE WHEN I AM BEING EFFECTIVE AS A FACILITATOR FOR THIS WORK?

Your feedback comes quickly and frequently quite directly from your students. The feedback typically includes:

🔳 Your students note that they feel relaxed.

🔳 Tensions in the room are noticeably lowered.

🔳 Students note an increased ability to reduce incessant monkey-mind chatter.

🔳 Students note an improved flow of imagery with the ability to experience more vivid images and understand their personal meaning.

🔳 Students exhibit an increased "presence."

🔳 After several weeks of using the exercises, students remind you to guide them in a relaxation and centering session if you forget to do so.

🔳 Students pay attention and focus more effectively on schoolwork.

TIPS FOR INDIVIDUAL USE OF DIRECTED IMAGERY

1. Practice on awakening and when preparing to go to sleep.
2. Make sure your body is comfortable.
3. Place your thumb, middle, and index fingers together.
4. Take several full breaths.
5. Focus inwardly for a minute or so.
6. Identify the problem or issue that you wish to announce to the brain. Using the two-screen technique, announce the issue, surrounded by a dark border on the first screen. Erase the image and then announce the desired outcome, surrounded by a luminous border, on the second screen. Hold that second screen image for a few seconds, until you can put strong positive feelings with it, then allow it to fade.
7. Focus on the quality of good feelings from the last image and hold it for a minute or so.
8. Return your focus to the aware state, or fall off to sleep.
9. Anytime you think of it, image yourself in a setting that signifies success for you.

ITEM 4: LETTER TO PARENTS

Following your study of this book and the accompanying audiocassettes, when you feel ready to begin using some simple image/relaxation exercises with your class, it will be helpful to send a copy of the letter on page 147 or your own version to parents to elicit their cooperation and support.

ITEM 5: USES FOR MUSIC IN THE CLASSROOM

I strongly recommend that you use music in the classroom in a planned fashion as part of your environment designed for learning. Living organisms are bio-oscillators. Our cells, individually and collectively, vibrate with sound and are affected by sounds. Sounds can either enhance or inhibit learning.

What this information will mean for you as an educator is a commitment to explore the use of music in the classroom for its possible benefits to enhance your own style of running

Dear Parent:

Stress and tension seem to affect us all. They can be upsetting to our health, happiness, and productivity. Students in the classroom are particularly susceptible to stress: many people are confined to limited space with limited opportunity to deal with excessive stressors.

Brain research confirms that as stress increases, the ability to learn decreases. Teachers hardly need research findings to know the effects on teaching of classroom-based tensions as well as those brought to the classroom via personal issues in students' lives. Research findings also confirm that learning can accelerate dramatically when teachers are trained in stress management skills such as those used extensively in business, industry, sport training, and medicine.

Having recently completed a training program in stress management with a focus on classroom use, I am pleased that our students can benefit from a group of simple yet highly effective exercises.

These relaxation and stress-release exercises not only open the door to better performance in school, but can translate into more cooperative and relaxed home experiences as well.

The exercises themselves involve procedures that you may already be using in your own lives, such as taking a few deep breaths when you feel tense, allowing body muscles to relax, and imagining a calm scene.

If your child tells you of such experiences in the classroom, you will appreciate knowing that the benefits of scientific research in improving learning are at work to help your child learn and perform at higher levels.

a learning center. You will likely become familiar with a wider range of music and sound than those you use for personal enjoyment. We will try to entice you by noting that the exploration can be great fun, add to your personal enjoyment of music, and become delightfully contagious, particularly if other educators in your school share this interest so that you can compare observations of what works in what settings.

You might consider the following:

1. Low-volume background classical music during student and your presentations
2. Slow largo movements from classical pieces for brainstorming and problem-solving sessions
3. Popular music for celebration of successes, sunny days, upcoming holidays, completion of units and lessons, and so on.
4. Daily fanfare for welcoming students into the classroom
5. Fanfare for introduction for students who are giving presentations
6. A variety of music for creating a mood: quieting or raising the energy level in the classroom
7. Bright, active music for movement: stretching; prelesson; switching focus; getting, bringing, making, cleaning-up exercises; working off excess steam
8. Start of class session: everyday opening; start of term, week, seasons of year; special days, including birthdays; victories in school-based activities
9. Music relating to emotions: fear, joy, calm, excitement, anger, sadness, and so on, for prewriting or acting moods
10. Storytelling, background to all positive-outcome patterning work. Use largo movements from classical compositions here.
11. Quiet time: during in-class study as well as during quizzes to help students recall information taken on board when music was first played

For general classroom use, I recommend that you allow students to choose some pop music to play. Play the music during active periods only, including entrance to class, movement, transitions, clean-ups, and leaving class.

After a week or two of such use, discuss with students how pop music is good for keeping them focused in *five-sense reality,* doing things actively in the world. Quiet music, on the other hand, can help them quiet their thoughts, help them to focus *inwardly* and *learn* more *easily* by learning to work from expanded brain modes. Then underscore the observation that fast-paced and heavy-beat music can be great for body movement but happens to be terrible for taking on board new information and getting it stored in long-term memory. For that purpose, slow-paced music with a light beat works beautifully. Therefore, the next series of music you will introduce them to will have nothing to do with pop music because such music is designed for movement and to draw attention to lyrics, beat, and melody, all of which is contrary to what is needed for learning in school. If you are ready to have your students put the material they learn into songs and rap, however, the pop music works just fine. Advise students that we have an extensive repertoire of music that can help them do better academically, improve their performance in sports, and generally learn anything more effortlessly with no effort on their parts at all.

Invite students to experiment for a week or two with having quiet music played in the background while they are doing schoolwork. During this experimental period, you will invite their feedback regarding what they notice about how they feel and work while this music is playing.

If you are so inclined, you can make an entire unit on the use of sound to enhance learning, and there is a significant body of literature to support this enhancement (see bibliography). Or you can do some preparation yourself and play different types of music for the students and have them get in touch with the feelings invoked by the different selections. You might make an audiocassette with marches, waltzes, fanfares, quiet guitar music, folk dances. American Indian chants, Buddhist monk chants, Pacific Islanders songs (Cook or Hawai'ian Islands are good choices), classical strings music, hunting melodies played on brass instruments; Mozart's German dances, Bartok's Hungarian dances, Dvorak's Romanian dances, Mozart's *A Musical Joke,* and Schubert's Trout Quintet. This project is an excellent one for your students, individually or in groups, to do; they will likely come up with additional suggestions.

We tend to teach in the way we ourselves learn. If you have taken Dunn and Dunn's Individual Learning Styles Preference Survey, for example, you can appreciate how we tend to set up our classrooms and teach the way *we* learn. Some readers will be *auditorially* oriented and will feel very comfortable using sound in the classroom. Tactile-kinesthetic learners should also be quite comfortable with music. The visual learner might tend to prefer visual stimuli, such as white-board work, posters, signs, bulletin boards, artwork, graphs, pictures, and so on, to auditory stimuli. With the fine body of literature validating the use of music in learning, we invite you to explore it, irrespective of your own learning style, to better provide environmental options to all learners passing through your particular learning environment.

SELECTION RECOMMENDATIONS

Once you put together a sample tape such as the one suggested above, you can add selections to each category so you have a handy library from which to select music for various moods and purposes. For general classwork, I highly recommend the string chamber music of Mozart and Hayden. The quartets and trios are available on CD and you can tape selections of slower movements.

ITEM 6

Our intention is to publish in the future a book of teacher- and student-generated story lines and applications of imagery to real-life situations and school achievement. We welcome your contributions and will identify them as such in the publication. Write to the author at 7096 Red Cedar Cove, Excelsior, MN 55331.

GLOSSARY

The *Magical Classroom* is designed not to be a theoretical treatise but rather a practical manual for facilitating expanded learning potential. We are interested in what works and in presenting skills critical to expand and accelerate learning, skills that educators can readily learn then facilitate in others.

Challenge learning: Name given to a combined teaching approach that utilizes the format of solving real-life problems, theme teaching, positive-outcome patterning, and lessons and activities to communicate desired positive outcomes to the brain.

Integrative learning: Actively accessing and applying resources of both brain hemispheres and the fuller spectrum of brain frequency functions.

Positive-outcome patterning: Term that denotes the positive utilization of an innate body/mind patterning process.

Stacking: Utilization of multiple learning-enhancing factors to facilitate maximal expansion of learning and performance.

BIBLIOGRAPHY

Armstrong, T. 1985. *The Radiant Child*. Wheaton, Ill.: Quest.

———. 1987. *In Their Own Way: Discovering and Encouraging Your Child's Personal Learning Style*. Los Angeles: J.P. Tarcher.

———. 1989. *Growing Up Creative*. New York: Crown.

Bandler, R. 1985. *Using Your Brain for a Change*. Moab, Utah: Real People.

Barbe, W. B., and R. H. Swassing. 1988. *Teaching through Modality Strengths: Concepts and Practices*. Columbus, Ohio: Zaner-Bloser.

Barth, R. S. 1991. *Improving Schools from Within*. San Francisco: Jossey-Bass.

Bettelheim, Bruno, and Karen Zelan. 1982. *On Learning to Read: The Child's Fascination with Meaning*. New York: Knopf.

Block, J. W., and L. W. Anderson. 1975. *Mastery Learning in Classrooms*. New York: Macmillan.

Bohm, D., and F. D. Peat. 1987. *Science Order and Creativity*. Toronto: Bantam.

Borysenko, J. 1987. *Minding the Body, Mending the Mind*. Reading, Mass.: Addison-Wesley.

Brandt, R. S., ed. 1992. *Performance Assessment*. Alexandria, Va.: Association for Supervision and Curriculum Development.

Bruner, J. 1986. *Actual Minds, Possible Worlds*. Cambridge, Mass.: Harvard University Press.

Bry, A. 1978. *Visualization: Directing the Movies of Your Mind*. New York: Harper and Row.

Burns, M. 1976. *The Book of Think: Or How to Solve a Problem Twice Your Size*. Boston: Little, Brown.

Buzan, T. 1988. *Make the Most of Your Mind*. London: Pan Books.

Caine, R. N., and G. Caine. 1991. *Making Connections: Teaching and the Human Brain*. Alexandria, Va.: Association for Supervision and Curriculum Development.

Campbell, B., L. Campbell, and D. Dickinson. 1992. *Teaching and Learning through Multiple Intelligences*. Seattle: New Horizons for Learning.

Campbell, D. G. 1983. *Introduction to the Musical Brain*. St. Louis, Mo.: MMB Music.

———. 1989. *The Roar of Silence*. Wheaton, Ill.: Theosophical Publishing.

Canfield, J., and H. C. Well. 1976. *100 Ways to Enhance Self-Esteem in the Classroom*. Englewood Cliffs, N.J.: Prentice Hall.

Carbo, M., R. Dunn, and K. Dunn. 1986. *Teaching Children to READ through Their Individual Learning Styles*. Englewood Cliffs, N.J.: Prentice Hall.

Chafetz, M. D. 1992. *Smart for Life*. New York: Penguin.

Chance, P. 1986. *Thinking in the Classroom*. New York: Teachers College Press.

Chopra, D. 1991 *Unconditional Life: Mastering the Forces that Shape Personal Reality*. New York: Bantam.

Clynes, M. 1982. *Music, Mind, and Brain: The Neuropsychology of Music*. New York: Plenum Press.

Comer, J. 1987. "New Haven's School-Community Connection." *Educational Leadership* 44, 6: 13–16.

Costa, A. 1991. *The School as a Home for the Mind*. Palatine, Ill.: Skylight.

Cremin, L. A. 1990. *Popular Education and Its Discontents*. New York: Harper and Row.

Csikszentmihalyi, M. 1990. *Flow: The Psychology of Optimal Experience*. New York: Harper and Row.

Dadd, D. L. 1986. *The Nontoxic Home*. Los Angeles: J. P. Tarcher.

David, J., and S. Peterson. 1984. *Can Schools Improve Themselves? A Study of School-Based Improvement Programs*. Palo Alto, Calif.: Bay Area Research Group.

Davidson, N., and T. Worsham. 1992. *Enhancing Thinking through Cooperative Learning*. New York: Teachers College Press.

DeMille, R. 1981. *Put Your Mother on the Ceiling: Children's Imagination Games*. Santa Barbara, Calif.: Santa Barbara Press.

Dennison, G. S. 1980. *The Lives of Children: The Story of the First Street School*. New York: Random House.

Dewey, J. 1933. *How We Think*. Rev. ed. New York: Heath.

Dhority, L. 1991. *The Act Approach: The Artful Use of Suggestion for Integrative Learning*. Bremen, Germany: PLS Verlag.

Diamond, M. 1987. *Enriching Heredity: The Impact of the Environment on the Anatomy of the Brain*. New York: The Free Press.

Diaz, A. 1992. *Freeing the Creative Spirit: Drawing on the Power of Art to Tap the Magic and Wisdom Within*. San Francisco: Harper.

Dunn, R., K. Dunn, and D. Treffinger. 1992. *Bringing Out the Giftedness in Your Child*. New York: John Wiley and Sons.

Dunn, K., and R. Dunn. 1992. *Teaching Elementary Students through Their Individual Learning Styles*. Needham Heights, Mass.: Allyn and Bacon.

Edwards, B. 1986. *Drawing on the Artist Within*. New York: Simon and Schuster.

Eisner, E. 1991. "What Really Counts in Schools." *Educational Leadership* 48, 5: 10–17.

Elkins, S. P. 1985. *Glad to Be Me: Building Self-Esteem in Yourself and Others*. Rochester, N.Y.: Growth Association.

Ellison, L. 1993. *Seeing with Magic Glasses*. Arlington, Va.: Great Ocean.

Elmore, R. F. 1992. "Why Restructuring Alone Won't Improve Teaching." *Educational Leadership* 49, 7: 44–48.

Epstein, G. 1989. *Healing Visualizations: Creating Health through Imagery*. New York: Bantam.

Fiske, E. B. 1991. *Smart Schools, Smart Kids*. New York: Simon and Schuster.

Forman, G., and D. Kuschner. 1977. *The Child's Construction of Knowledge: Piaget for Teaching Children*. Belmont, Calif.: Wadworth.

Frith, T. 1985. *Secrets Parents Should Know about Public Schools*. New York: Simon and Schuster.

Fugit, E. 1982. *He Hit Me Back First! Creative Visualization Activities for Parenting and Teaching*. Rolling Hills Estates, Calif.: Jalmar.

Fullan, M. G., and S. Steigelbauer. 1991. *The New Meaning of Educational Change*. New York: Teachers College Press.

Gardner, H. 1983. *Frames of Mind: The Theory of Multiple Intelligences*. New York: Basic.

———. 1991. *The Unschooled Mind*. New York: Basic.

Gatto, J. T. 1992. *Dumbing Us Down*. Philadelphia: New Society.

Gazzaniga, M. 1985. *The Social Brain: Discovering the Networks of the Mind*. New York: Basic.

Glasser, William. 1969. *Schools without Failure*. New York: Harper and Row.

———. 1990. *The Quality School*. New York: Harper and Row.

Glickman, C. D. 1993. *Renewing America's Schools: A Guide for School-Based Action*. San Francisco: Jossey-Bass.

Goldberg, P. 1983. *The Intuitive Edge*. Los Angeles: J. P. Tarcher.

Goodlad, J. 1984. *A Place Called School*. New York: McGraw-Hill.

Greene, L. J. 1987. *Smarter Kids*. New York: Fawcett Crest.

Gross, R. 1991. *Peak Learning*. Los Angeles, J. P. Tarcher.

Hadamard, J. 1945. *An Essay on the Psychology of Invention in the Mathematical Field*. Princeton, N.J.: Princeton University Press.

Halpern, S., and L. Savary. 1985. *Sound Health: The Music and Sounds that Make Us Whole*. San Francisco: Harper and Row.

Harman, W., and H. Rheingold. 1984. *Higher Creativity: Liberating the Unconscious for Breakthrough Insights*. Los Angeles, J. P. Tarcher.

Hart, L. 1975. *How the Brain Works*. New York: Basic.

Healy, J. M. 1987. *Your Child's Growing Mind*. New York: Doubleday.

———. 1990. *Endangered Minds: Why Children Don't Think and What We Can Do about It*. New York: Simon and Schuster.

Hendricks, G., and T. Roberts. 1977. *The Second Centering Book: More Awareness Activities for Children, Parents, and Teachers*. Englewood Cliffs, N.J.: Prentice-Hall.

Herbert, N. 1985. *Quantum Reality*. New York: Doubleday.

Herzog, S. 1982. *Joy in the Classroom*. Boulder Creek, Calif.: University of the Trees Press.

Holt, J. 1981. *Teach Your Own*. New York: Delacorte, Seymour Lawrence.

———. 1989. *Learning All the Time*. New York: Addison-Wesley.

Hunter, M. 1969. *Teach More Faster!* El Segundo, Calif.: TIP.

———. 1982. *Mastery Teaching*. El Segundo, Calif.: TIP.

James, M., and D. Jongeward. 1978. *Born to Win*. New York: New American Library.

Jenkins, J., ed. 1988. *Teachers as Advisors Program: Evaluation Report*. Tallahassee, Fla.: Florida State Department of Education.

Johnson, D. W., and R. T. Johnson. 1994. *The New Circles of Learning: Cooperation in the Classroom and School*. Alexandria, Va.,: Association for Supervision and Curriculum Development.

Judy, S. 1990. *Making Music for the Joy of It*. Los Angeles,: J. P. Tarcher.

Katz, L., and S. Chard. 1989. *Engaging Children's Minds: The Project Approach*. New York: Ablex.

Klein, P. 1988. *The Everyday Genius*. New York: Great Ocean.

Knowles, M. 1983. *Self-Directed Learning*. New York: Association Press.

Kohl, H. 1974. *Math, Writing, and Games in the Open Classroom*. New York: Random House.

Laborde, G. Z. 1988. *Fine Tune Your Brain*. Palo Alto, Calif.: Syntony.

Lakoff, G. 1980. *Metaphors We Live By*. Chicago: University of Chicago Press.

Lazear, D. 1991. *Seven Ways of Teaching*. Palatine, Ill.,: Skylight.

Leonard, G. 1987. *Education and Ecstasy and the Great School Reform Hoax*. Berkeley, Calif.: North Atlantic Books.

LePage, A. 1987. *Transforming Education: The New 3 Rs*. Oakland, Calif.: Oakmore House.

Leuner, H. 1984. *Guided Affective Imagery*. New York: Thieme-Stratton.

Levine, D. U. 1991. "Creating Effective Schools: Findings and Implications from Research and Practice." *Phi Delta Kappan 72*, 5: 389–93.

Lingerman, H. A. 1983. *The Healing Energies of Music*. Wheaton, Ill.: Quest Books.

Lozanov, G. 1978. *Suggestology and Outlines of Suggestopedy*. New York: Gordon and Breach.

Machado, L. A. 1980. *The Right to Be Intelligent*. Elmsford, N.Y.: Pergamon.

Markova, D. 1992. *How Your Child Is Smart*. Emeryville, Calif.: Conari Press.

Martz, L. 1992. *Making Schools Better*. New York: Times Books.

Marzano, R. J. 1992. *A Different Kind of Classroom: Teaching with Dimensions of Learning*. Alexandria, Va.: Association for Supervision and Curriculum Development.

Maslow, A. H. 1968. *Toward a Psychology of Being*. New York: Van Nostrand Reinhold.

McCarthy, B. 1980. *The 4MAT System*. Oak Harbor, Ill.: Excel.

McGuire, J. 1985. *Creative Storytelling: Choosing, Inventing, and Sharing Tales for Children*. New York: McGraw-Hill.

McKim, R. H. 1980. *Experiences in Visual Thinking*. Monterrey, Calif.: Brooks Cole.

Miller, J. P. 1988. *The Holistic Curriculum*. Toronto: OISE Press.

Miller, R. 1990. *What Are Schools For?: Holistic Education in American Culture*. Brandon, Vt.: Holistic Education Press.

Montessori, M. 1989. *The Absorbent Mind*. New York: Delta.

Nathan, J., ed. 1988. *Public Schools by Choice*. Bloomington, Ind.: Meyer Stone Books.

Neil, A. S. 1984. *Summerhill*. New York: Pocket.

Newman, J. M., ed. 1985. *Whole Language: Theory in Use*. Portsmouth, N.H. Heinemann.

Noddings, N., and P. Shore. 1984. *Awakening the Inner Eye: Intuition in Education*. New York: Teachers College Press.

Oakes, J. 1985. *Keeping Track: How Schools Structure Inequality*. New Haven, Conn.: Yale University Press.

Ornstein, R., and D. Sobel. 1987. *The Healing Brain: Breakthrough Discoveries about How the Brain Keeps Us Healthy*. New York: Simon and Schuster.

Ott, J. N. 1985. *Light, Radiation, and You: How to Stay Healthy*. Greenwich, Conn.: Devin-Adair.

Pearce, J. C. 1977. *Magical Child*. New York: E. P. Dutton.

Perkins, D. 1992. *Smart Schools: From Training Memories to Educating Minds*. New York: The Free Press.

Perone, V., ed. 1991. *Expanding Student Assessment*. Alexandria, Va.: Association for Supervision and Curriculum Development.

Piaget, J. H. 1952. *The Origins of Intelligence in Children*. New York: Norton.

———. 1954. *The Construction of Reality in the Child*. New York: Basic Books.

———. 1974. *To Understand Is to Invent: The Future of Education*. New York: Grossman.

Prigogine, I. 1980. *From Being to Becoming: Time and Complexity in the Physical Sciences*. San Francisco: W. H. Freeman.

Richards, M. C. 1980. *Toward Wholeness: Rudolf Steiner Education in America*. Middletown, Conn.: Wesleyan University Press.

Rico, G. L. 1983. *Writing the Natural Way: Using Right Brain Techniques to Release Your Expressive Powers*. Los Angeles: J. P. Tarcher.

Rowland, S. 1984. *The Inquiring Classroom: An Approach to Understanding Children's Learning*. London: Falmer Press.

Samples, R. F. 1976. *The Metaphorical Mind*. Reading, Mass.: Addison-Wesley.

Samuels, M., and N. Samuels. 1975. *Seeing with the Mind's Eye: The History, Techniques, and Uses of Visualization*. New York: Random House, Bookworks.

Satir, V. 1988. *The New Peoplemaking*. Moutain View, Calif.: Science and Behavior books.

Saunders, A., and B. Remsberg. 1986. *The Stress-Proof Child*. New York: Signet.

Schuster, D. H., and C. E. Gritton. 1986. *Suggestive Accelerative Learning Techniques*. New York: Gordon and Breach.

Seeley, M. M. 1994. "The Mismatch between Assessment and Grading." *Educational Leadership 52*, 2: 4–6.

Selye, H. 1976. *Stress Without Distress*. New York: McGraw-Hill.

Shorr, J. E. 1985. *Go See the Movies in Your Head*. Santa Barbara, Calif.: Ross-Erickson.

Singer, J. L., and Switzer, E. 1980. *Mind-Play: The Creative Uses of Fantasy*. Englewood Cliffs, N.J.: Prentice-Hall.

Sizer, T. R. 1992a. *Horace's Dream*. Boston: Houghton Mifflin.

———. 1992b. *Horace's School: Redesigning of the American High School*. New York: Houghton Mifflin.

Slavin, R. E. 1990. *Cooperative Learning Theory, Research, and Practice*. Englewood Cliffs, N.J.: Prentice-Hall.

Slavin, R., M. Karweit, and B. Wasik. 1992. "Preventing Early School Failure." *Educational Leadership 50,* 4: 10–18.

Steiner, R. 1967. *The Younger Generation*. Spring Valley, N.Y.: Anthroposophic Press.

Sternberg, R. 1985. *Beyond IQ*. New York: Cambridge University Press.

Stoddard, L. 1992. *Redesigning Education: A Guide for Developing Human Greatness*. Tucson, Ariz.: Zephyr Press.

Suzuki, S. 1982. *Nurtured by Love: New Approach to Education*. Pompano Beach, Fla.: Exposition Press of Florida.

Tart, C. 1987. *Waking Up: Overcoming the Obstacles to Human Potential*. Boston: Shambhala.

Taylor, Shelley, and Jonathon Brown. 1988. *Psychological Bulletin 103:* 193–210.

Toch, T. 1991. *In the Name of Excellence: The Struggle to Reform the Nation's Schools, Why It's Failing, and What Should Be Done.* New York: Oxford University Press.

Tomatis, A. A. 1991. *The Conscious Ear.* Barrytown, N.Y.: Station Hill Press.

Vitale, B. M. 1985. *Unicorns Are Real: A Right-Brained Approach to Learning.* New York: Warner.

von Oech, R. 1983. *A Whack on the Side of the Head.* New York: Warner.

Warner, S. 1989. *Encouraging the Artist in Your Child.* New York: St. Martin's Press.

Wheelock, A. 1992. *Crossing the Tracks: How Untracking Can Save America's Schools.* New York: New Press.

Wiggington, E. 1986. *Sometimes a Shining Moment.* New York: Anchor Press, Doubleday.

Wiggins, G. 1989. "Teaching to the (Authentic) Test." *Educational Leadership 46,* 7: 41–47.

Williams, L. V. 1986. *Teaching for the Two-Sided Mind.* New York: Simon and Schuster.

Wonder, J., and P. Donovan. 1984. *Whole-Brain Thinking.* New York: William Morrow.

Wood, G. H. 1992. *Schools that Work: America's Most Innovative Public Education Programs.* New York: Dutton.

Wright, E. 1989. *Good Morning Class, I Love You.* Rolling Hills, Calif.: Jalmar Press.

Zdenek, M. 1987. *Inventing the Future.* New York: McGraw Hill.

Zukav, G. 1979. *The Dancing Wu Li Masters.* New York: Morrow.

NOTES

NOTES